The
Aspiring Manager's
Survival Guide

How to Achieve
Success and Career Fulfilment
in a Changing Workplace

Mike Johnson

Butterworth-Heinemann
Linacre House, Jordan Hill, Oxford OX2 8DP
313 Washington Street, Newton, MA 02158
A division of Reed Educational and Professional Publishing Ltd

ℛ A member of the Reed Elsevier plc group

OXFORD   BOSTON   JOHANNESBURG
MELBOURNE   NEW DELHI   SINGAPORE

First published 1996

British Library Cataloguing in Publication Data
A catalogue record for this book is available from the British Library

Library of Congress Cataloguing in Publication Data
A catalogue record for this book is available from the Library of Congress

ISBN 0 7506 2703 4

Printed in the United States of America

For more information about this and related business titles, contact:

Special Sales Manager
Butterworth-Heinemann
Linacre House, Jordan Hill
Oxford OX2 8DP

For information on all Business publications, contact our World Wide
Web home page:

In the USA, **http://www.bh.com**
In the UK, **http://WWW.heinemann.co.uk**

*This book is dedicated to all those seeking
to change their careers and their lives.
I hope it helps you to understand the changes
we have gone through and helps you achieve
what YOU—not THEY—want.*

Contents

Personal Thanks   *ix*

Introduction   *xi*

1. *Why Is There a New World of Work?*   *1*

2. *Taking Hold of Your Own Destiny:*
   Inside the Organization   *28*

3. *Getting It Together in the New Organizational*
   Framework   *54*

4. *Don't Wait for Someone Else to Help You*   *85*

5. *Getting Out*   *107*

6. *How to Get (re)Hired*   *129*

7. *So You Want to Go It Alone?*   *155*

8. *Checklists for Action*   *178*

Bibliography   *197*

Index   *198*

Personal Thanks

A lot of people go into making a book work, particularly any book that needs professional input to make it relevant. My thanks to all those who agreed to be interviewed, many of whose thoughts did not get quoted but helped build a picture of where our working world is today. Special thanks to three organizations: European Career Partners, and especially their president, Win Nystrom of PCM Europe in Brussels, for his unflagging help and assistance. Likewise, Career Counselors International in the United States for their help and encouragement—especially in agreeing to a mammoth three-hour group interview. Also, Neumann International and their president, Helmut Neumann, for special assistance and access to their client base. Several individuals also made this book possible: John Humble for correcting many of my early ideas, Tom Acuff of Neumann International for his input and much-needed enthusiasm, and Mike Staunton of Management Centre Europe for countless late-night counseling sessions. Finally, I thank Bodil Jones at Johnson & Associates for chasing down interviews and research input and correcting the manuscript; my grateful thanks to all of them.

Introduction

This book is two things: a requiem for yesterday's organizational culture and a celebration of the renaissance of the new working world order. Thankfully, it doesn't dwell for long on the former; it concentrates on what is happening now as we head through this period of transition into a new world of work. That is exactly what we are going through, and the smart managers—the trendsetters, the best and the brightest—have already seen that and have made the jump to the changed workplace.

What is it? What can you expect? Put simply, the new world of work requires more from you as an individual. Whether inside the organization or as a supplier of services, you will have to work smarter, know more, and keep on learning—not just in your profession but in other skills and processes as well, if you want to stay ahead of the rest.

Describing how that new working world is taking shape is the purpose of this book. By calling on some of the leading career counselors, management consultants, and human resource specialists, it has been possible to create a complete picture of tomorrow's working world, where you will fit in, and what you need in terms of knowledge and skills to get a membership card.

In the past, people who had made it were said to have "had their ticket punched in all the right places." That is also true today. But the ticket is different, and the holes are in other places. Essentially, all we have done is move the punch holes around, creating a world of work where there is more freedom, more creativity, and more opportunity than ever before. Now there are a lot more places that you need to have that ticket punched—a lot more skills and experience that are required—before you are able to take your place in the new work order.

Certainly in reading this book no one should despair. Of course, change is all around us and we are going to have to adapt. But change can be stimulating and it can be fun; it doesn't have to be fraught with anxiety and fear. Most of all, what I set out to do was to show how the new world of work isn't a fearsome place at all but a great opportunity for all of us who have to work for a living so we may enjoy earning our daily bread.

Interestingly, what this book also shows is the different ways that North America, Europe, and parts of Asia are tackling these major changes. While social and cultural issues may color how executive work patterns are changing, there is much that is common in recognizing what we still have to do in getting our organizations into shape to meet these new challenges.

Finally, this book is designed to be a practical tool, a self-help guide for all of us in this new age. First, it will help those who want to stay in the organization by showing how work is changing and how they can be a part of that revolution. Second, it gives advice for those who want to change jobs, outlining what they must do to be employable. Third, it shows redundant executives who want to get rehired what kind of organization they can expect to find and how to get to the front of the hiring line. Finally, for those who want to go it alone, it offers some sound advice on what and—more important—what not to do.

There are three elements designed to make the book as practical as possible.

First, throughout the text you will find globe icons with boxed text. These emphasize key points and issues.

Second, there is a summary at the end of each chapter of Key Points, ending with a "What You Should Do Now" checklist, to help you assess yourself as you work through the book.

Third, the final chapter (chapter 8) is a series of checklists to help you assess yourself, your organization, and your entrepreneurial abilities.

These checklists at the end of each chapter and in chapter 8 have been laid out so that you can easily begin to use them while you are on the move. As lots of business books are bought in bus and railroad terminals and airports or read in hotel rooms, the checklists have been put together so they are easy to read and will trigger new ideas and help focus your thoughts. All the same, solo assessments are not recommended. As the book continuously repeats, check out your ideas with close friends or trusted work colleagues. Get their input—it's important.

Wherever you read this book and whatever your situation, I hope that the collective wisdom presented here will help you develop and sustain a successful and fulfilling career- or job-getting campaign—in this new world of work.

Mike Johnson
Brussels, Belgium, June 1996

Why Is There a New World of Work?

What a man in the street wants is not a big debate on fundamental issues. He wants a little medical care, a rug on the floor, a picture on the wall, a little music in the house, and a place to take Molly and the grandchildren when he retires.

—LYNDON B. JOHNSON

Little by little, the pimps have taken over the world. They don't do anything, they don't make anything—they just stand there and take their cut.

—JEAN GIRAUDOUX

Let's begin with an old schoolboy joke:

- I've good news and bad news: which do you want to hear first?
- The good news.
- OK, you've only got forty-eight hours to live!
- Golly, if that's the good news, what's the bad news?
- I forgot to tell you yesterday!

For many executives, managers, supervisors, and specialists across most of what we call the Western developed economies, that joke has become all too real. For many of us have been systematically lied to, misled, or, at the very least, mismanaged, losing in the process chances we may have had to retarget or refocus our lives had we had the time to do so and the information to see it was going to be a necessity.

While organizations have gone into seemingly irreversible tail-spins, while shareholders have demanded more profits, while an increasingly large number of senior executives have been behaving like pigs with their noses snuffling up money in the corporate feeding trough, we mere workers have had to hang onto our hats, pull up our socks, and get on with it. And in most cases—in our ill-labeled developed economies—we have had to work harder, often for less, to increase productivity while covering the job of the dear departed: our former colleagues who have just been downsized, rightsized, and obliterated before our eyes.

Add to that an increasing burden brought about by little improvement in real wage and salary levels and almost universal governmental inability to retrain the workforce and it is clear that corporate greed, investor greed, and government inaction are fueling what could well be a coming social crisis. As more jobs are likely to go in the Western economies—with many of those the jobs of white-collar workers who, just a decade ago, thought themselves immune from such possibilities—the question that every concerned adult (indeed anyone over fifteen) should be asking is What are my personal prospects for the future and how do I ensure I can stay self-reliant and self-sufficient?

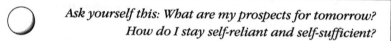

> *Ask yourself this: What are my prospects for tomorrow?*
> *How do I stay self-reliant and self-sufficient?*

On the downside, the answer is difficult, because it depends on so many elements—the country you live in, the qualifications and skills you have, your ability and willingness to relocate, the extent of your ambition, and the quality of life you want. On the upside, the answer is still not simple, but it is encouraging. There is a future out there, there is employment, there is challenge, there are excitement and fulfillment as well. What it takes is a recognition (an admission if you like) that the world is a changed place. The jobs that have gone have gone for good. The businesses that closed won't reopen. But we don't all have to end our lives as hamburger flippers—far from it. There are new jobs, new careers, outstanding new entrepreneurial activities. It isn't Armageddon; it's natural change, just as we changed from the agricultural age to the industrial age. Now the postindustrial society has already taken shape, and the best thing to do is join it, embrace it—or at least get to like it—because it's going to be around for a while.

This book sets out to chart a course through the new age, where knowledge (what you know, what's stored in your brain) is your personal gold card to success. Unlike the schoolboy story at the beginning, it has a happier ending.

My confidence in saying that is that I know the end already, and it is a lot more fun than the beginning. To focus your interest on finding out what happens, this book has been developed with the help of some of the world's leading outplacement, career management, executive search, and human resource experts, who gave their considerable expertise—but most importantly their day-to-day knowledge and observation of what's really what in the marketplace—to provide a real picture: a practical assessment, not a theory or an idea of what might be happening out there.

Their inputs and observations are the core of this book. Their thoughts about tomorrow's avenues of success and routes to the top are the most relevant anyone can get, because every day in life each and every one of them works with all the people who make up our business society today, whether in North America, Europe, or Asia. They see the changes, they know who wants what, where, and when. Those thoughts, which have been distilled into this book, are powerful pointers to tomorrow's new working world and how we all go about getting our share of the future.

However, to understand fully the ramifications of the change, we need to assess where we are right now. Where we are right now is in a considerable mess. A few industries apart, there's little growth and certainly zero growth in human terms. Head count got replaced by body count long ago, and the trend is continuing downward and is likely to stay that way in terms of permanent hires in the traditional industry giants (banks and finance services, heavy manufacturing, consumer goods producers). Additionally, in many countries (particularly those of a socialist persuasion in western Europe) there is little job creation in even small and medium-sized companies (SMEs), as the incentive to take on new hires is strongly diluted by hard-hitting social costs that burden even the most enthusiastic free marketer.

A lot of what has been happening and will continue to happen has been based on the ability of employees to fool themselves into not believing the worst and to find an assurance that everything will be all right. And this deceiving ourselves has often been quite easy to achieve, especially when chairmen—and I would suppose some chairwomen too—as well as presidents, managing directors, and owners of start-ups have in many cases told less than the truth as their organizations have chased more profit or hit the slippery slope of a market slump. Often getting out with millions or being re-

warded with stock option bonuses by delighted investors and external boards for the "creative" act of axing 20 percent of the workforce, these pillars of the industrial establishment have not given
those of us in the lower ranks much of a real picture—and certainly
little news about the future.

While there are organizations and individuals out there who care
and nurture their people, the 1990s have been illuminated by stories of business greed, undeserved bonuses, and, in some cases,
outright fraud. Additionally, as institutional shareholders demanded more returns, finding the fast, expedient way to better quar-
terly results became a norm. In doing this, many heads of business
kept up a propaganda line about how well the business was doing,
how no one was going to get fired, how we would all end up in an
organizational utopia. And we believed them!

Senior managers lied to middle managers. Middle managers lied
before they died. As reported *Fortune* magazine, "Companies used
reengineering to jackhammer out the middle-manager staircase."
Lower down, specialists and supervisors, wary that their jobs were
on the line, did nothing to change the status quo. They, in fooling
themselves that all would be well, gave those same rose-tinted as-
surances to any blue-collar worker who had the temerity to ask
what was going on.

What was going on was simple in the extreme to explain. As an
article in the United Kingdom's *Sunday Times* said, "The management culture that produces leaner, fitter, faster organizations, identified by professor Charles Handy in his book *The Empty Raincoat*,
has held sway. Handy's formula, that if you employ half the workforce but pay them twice as much they will be three times more productive, is chapter one, verse one of the modern management
handbook."

And in case anyone has the idea that not all companies are like
that, think again. Employers who gallantly held out against these
new forces found themselves unable to sustain market share and
had to follow the same cost-cutting, people-cutting exercises as the
rest, much as it may have pained them to do so. There was simply
no way to survive by being altruistic; the benevolent corporation
ceased to exist.

The demise, through hard-nosed market forces, of the more benevolent style of corporation has probably been the hardest to take.
Sadly, in some cases those with a keep-the-staff-at-any-price philosophy have created more pain for their people than the tough guys,
because often they failed to make deep enough cuts in the organi-

THE ALIENATED EMPLOYEE

Sometimes, there is just no way round it. Whether the company has at some time got it wrong, or you just hired badly, there is a category of employee that you just can't seem to help—the classic victim of the new working world, who—whether victim of poor development or just someone with an attitude problem—will never, ever change. Adrian Furnham, professor of psychology at University College London, calls them "the alienated employees, cynical, unhelpful, and poisonous to those around them." These people are the first casualties of this battle for a new working world, and little, it seems, can be done to help them.

In today's madcap business world, says Furnham, "people become alienated for various reasons. Many fairly loyal, though hardly stretched, employees who had put in their years of service, supposedly secure in the knowledge that promotion and the good life would follow, suddenly feel let down. Like some Russians now calling for a return to the old certainties, alienated workers are past, not future, focused. They carry about the baggage of the past, trapped by its false promises."

Furnham suggests that these people "represent the quit-but-stay types, who choose not to leave their changing organization but continue in the new role or job with the old habits." They are usually, claims Furnham, "middle-aged, not particularly well educated, and may never have worked for another company. Their inflexibility, unwillingness to adapt, and continual sourness are a major headache for companies trying to reinvent themselves."

According to Furnham, there are three routes to ridding organizations of this type of worker.

One: Buy them out. It may seem costly in the short term, but it may be the best solution. Everyone has his or her price, and if the company is prepared to throw in some outplacement counseling, even the most security-minded employee might be prepared to leap into the job pool. Most are frightened (even more than the rest of us) of what they perceive to be the icy-cold, shark-infested waters of the commercial world. The company environment—however much it has changed—still looks warm and protective. To sell the concept of a leaving package you need to reverse these perceptions, pointing out how cold and competitive the company must become and how warm and rosy the opportunities are out there in the real world.

Two: Raise the game. Quit-but-stayers need to know that there are significant changes in the way things are done in the new organization. The talk of revenue-up, cost-down, lean-and-mean organizations needs to be supported by tougher targets for individual workers. There are various ways to raise the game that include changing equipment to that new technology that has to be mastered, removing or reducing support staff and functions, or more simply demanding more productivity. The thought of having to put in more effort perpetually frequently frightens off alienated individuals, or they change into productive and committed workers.

Three: Introduce new blood. This more risky strategy involves bringing in new (mostly young) people with no memory of the past. Forward-looking, enthusiastic, and manageable, new people soon show up the alienated workers. To these people the alienated workers often appear more pathetic than wise, and their ostracism by the young and upwardly mobile may either succeed in scaring them off or changing them." Warns Furnham, "The alienated worker is a menace to the organization and him or herself. They need either to learn to adapt to new conditions, to recognize the new world as it is, or quit the workplace."

Tough talk perhaps. But unless you can change the mind-set of people like this they have to be considered high atop the list of dead or missing in the coming business battles for tomorrow's corporate high ground.

zation and had to come back time and time again—a recipe that ensures a constant culture of fear and bewilderment. In some companies this constant hacking at more and more departments became known by the acronym B-O-H-I-C-A, meaning "bend over, here it comes again."

Even the so-called corporate press, the management and business magazines, couldn't stop commenting on what was happening in their midst. As the U.K.'s leading executive monthly *Management Today* tartly observed, "Welcome to the nightmare of an entire generation of forty-five-plus middle-class managers who woke up one morning to find that the contract they thought they had signed up to—steady employment with regular promotions in a big organization, the contract that guaranteed them identity and status—had been torn up overnight."

Comments U.S. management expert Mike Kami, "Reorganizing, downsizing, reengineering, consolidating, and streamlining are not meaningless buzzwords to millions of employees who permanently lost their jobs. Some are still unemployed; most had to settle for lower-paying positions. They had to decrease their living standards and drastically change their retirement plans." Kami adds, "This new reality also deeply affected the employees who were not affected by the layoffs. The survivors are scared and bitter. They may not show it, but their priorities and attitudes changed. There is a significant reduction of employee loyalty, dedication, entrepreneurship, and innovation. There is a significant increase of self-protection, playing it safe and looking for other opportunities, while still on the job. The overall morale has decreased and so has management's credibility."

So much has management's credibility been blown asunder that there is now a new level of mistrust among those left in the middle ranks. As a professor who teaches a mature MBA class reports, "The cynicism amongst the class is incredible; their attitude is if the boss is stealing so can they. This does not augur well for our corporations of the future."

Simon Caulkin, writing in *Management Today*, concurs. "Not surprisingly, beneath the enthusiastic whitewash of the human resource specialists (who use words like 'empowerment,' 'teamwork,' and 'alignment') dysfunctionalities abound. If they were people, a number of leading organizations would be institutionalized." Caulkin goes on to explain that "many chief executives, usually happier communicating with investors than their own staff, are operating in increasing isolation from reality: while they savor plaudits from shareholders for the hard-nosed heroics that have kept the company afloat through recession, they are sitting atop a seething heap of managerial fear and loathing that threatens to nullify all their efforts at boosting productivity."

So, in ten short, hectic years the world of work has changed completely. There is no career path, no job security, and for those of us still in work, the pressure of having to do two and even three people's jobs, while still scared we may lose ours as well, is an everyday, stressful reality. While all that is happening we are being asked to smile and say "thank you" as well.

In some cases, we could be forgiven for assuming we were headed for a new working world that comprised the very best of Dickensian employment practices. As an article by Will Hutton in the *Guardian* newspaper in the United Kingdom points out, "Companies can more profitably manage the ebb and flow of demand over the business cycle if they reduce their core staff to a minimum and hire additional workers on contracts. The famous example is Burger King, where young workers clocked on when customers appeared; this reduced their wages to a derisory level but ensured they were only paid for the minutes they were needed."

The executive classes are affected as well in what are often less than laudatory strategy moves. A multinational chemical concern moved its German headquarters across the country. Lots of executives didn't or wouldn't come along, so they paid them off and lowered the average age level by seven years in one stroke. Now they have a younger, lower-paid workforce. This has also happened in France with corporations heading out of Paris for some new retreat in the countryside; even *La Belle France* has been looking exceedingly ugly.

Many people are beginning to question not only the morality but also the rationality of the cut, cut, cut, performance-at-any-price management style that has characterized the last decade. Indeed there are still some of us left who remember that the old form of the business community went beyond just work. It was a social organization that established and embraced people. It was one of the three pillars of our Western existence (family and community were the other two, and of course you could add religion or leisure pursuits if you are so inclined), and its loss has wrenched out more than just a name on a salary slip.

> *The business community should still go beyond just work: it should be a social organization that establishes and embraces people.*

Robin Linnecar, a career consultant with KPMG, suggests that the changes may have gone too far. "We've developed a situation where you either have one and a half jobs or you have none. This is not sustainable. Organizations will discover that simply getting the head count down and working people too much is not efficient. And there will be a backlash from people. They are going to be saying increasingly, 'I'm not going to do that.' "

An ex-editor of *Fortune*, Jack Patterson, writing in his former magazine, adds to that thought: "The danger I see is that the intangible but indispensable values I discovered at work will be lost, the sense of community, the shared goals, the spirited exchange of ideas, the pride of achievement. They are not, I admit, the concepts managers generally use to measure employee performance, but without them I think that permanent increases in efficiency and quality will be difficult or impossible to achieve."

Of course the other thing that they are both saying between the lines is that this work revolution went further up the organizational ladder than ever before. Middle managers got affected; that meant the middle class got affected. They are bruised and battered and they don't like it one bit; there is strong evidence that they feel that things have gone too far already. Worse still, in many organizations, senior managers, sometimes very senior managers, were falling out of the sky as well. So the worry is universal. It's not just those blue collars anymore, it's everyone. As a recently reengineered middle manager comments, "Look at your CEO. Look behind the mask, you may well find that he or she—in reality—is more uneasy than you are."

CEOs have good reason to be uneasy. As many experts have commented, the problems that arose were based on the inability of many senior managers to see the signs, read the cards, or look into the crystal ball. The emergence of world markets—bringing with them new, unheard-of competitors—and rapid switches in global economies all needed keen, sharp-eyed observers to predict what was coming next. What a lot of organizations didn't have were senior managers who could recognize that the game had changed not for a few years but forever. In some ways it is difficult to lay the blame solely at their door; they just didn't have the market intelligence to meet the future and they collided head-on. As everyone who has seen a traffic accident knows, head-on collisions are messy—no wonder top management is walking around frightened and worried as well.

So, if we are all frightened, where do we go from here? First, we have to recognize that a lot of what has been going on is, quite possibly, counterproductive, but there's not much we can do about that; hindsight is not a very practical tool. Second, we have to realize that the effects of this madcap rush to eliminate whole levels of the workforce are equivalent to a war: there are dead and wounded lying all over the place and, hard as it is, we have to accept that as well, no matter how unpalatable it may be. Third, in the process of getting all of us back on track again we have to also accept that traditional jobs have gone forever and we are already in a new age where we will need more skills, we will need to stay aware of new ideas and developments, and we cannot plan for a job for life. Finally, we have to get it through our heads that, just as in a shooting war, there are victims, people with their name on a bullet, who are not going to change, not going to adapt, and will fall by the wayside. Thinking that this change in the way we work is a temporary aberration is foolish and will get us absolutely nowhere.

John Doerr is managing director of Management Centre Europe (MCE) in Brussels, Europe's leading management development and information provider. He stated, "There will be victims in this transitional period, much like we saw as Western society evolved from a farm economy to an industrial one; they are victims of history's inexorable tide forward. We can wail and gnash our teeth, but the reality is that many people can't move to find the next job, nor can they acquire the necessary skills, nor do they have the ability."

Australian consultant Tony Randall, a director of Management Frontiers in Sydney, concurs and offers a brutal truth: "Those who are not fitted mentally or emotionally to the environment of the new working world have two choices. One, they can be helped to adjust by government or business-funded training, advisory, and support schemes. Two, they have to accept a reduced material standard of living by moving or undertaking work that is not mentally or emotionally disturbing, like moving from the competitive world of the big city to the quieter life of a rural community."

Linda Holbeche, director of research at Roffey Park Management Institute in the United Kingdom, is also firm on the issue of victims of change: "For those not fitted out for this brave new world, the options seem pretty bleak to me. It looks as though they will opt—wrongly—for increasing conformism or specialization in the hope this will ensure job security."

> *It isn't the strongest, the richest, or the best educated who will win, but those with the mental muscle to embrace change.*

Lecturer and author of the hugely successful book *How to Use Your Head* Tony Buzan makes another point about victims and adds some data about survivors: "Yes, this transition we are going through will cause casualties. But, recent surveys of people that survive natural disasters, shipwrecks, earthquakes, and so on have shown an extraordinary correlation between those that thought they would live and did so and those that thought they would die—and did just that. Eyewitness survivors report people who give up easily without a fight, indeed people who were happy to go." Buzan's thought, therefore, is that "during this transition we are going through, the survival process and that of being a victim are purely mental—purely states of mind. Those that want to exist, want to succeed, will; others will just give up and metaphorically drown."

THE HEAD-COUNT MYTH

There have been press articles suggesting that after lopping off corporate bark and branches willy-nilly, corporations have got themselves in an employee shortage fix and are starting to rehire. Not so, say search consultants around the globe. A poll conducted specially for this book by Neumann International in Europe and its global partners, MRI in the United States and Morgan and Banks in Asia, found zero evidence that this was in any way true. What was happening in industries that had evolved into new areas or thrown off the shackles of recession was new hiring of new people in new jobs.

As to whether the organizational pyramid is growing again, with axed-out levels being reinstated or re-created, there seems to be little evidence—despite all the rumor—that this is happening in real life. However, the Neumann investigation prompted an interesting comment by Andreas Durst, a business unit manager with AT&T in Europe. "I am convinced that rebuilding the pyramid has more to do with senior executive fear of becoming too measurable themselves: that is my view of the reason to rebuild middle management layers."

Bank of America's Jim Prouty looks at the rehiring issue in another way. "Sure we did downsize to the bone, but I honestly can't think of one example where we had to turn around and hire people because the cuts were too deep. However, cutting to the bone gives you a good opportunity to add the right resources selectively when new opportunities (not envisioned in the restructuring) arise."

Prouty goes on to explain the long-term advantage of this approach. "If we still had a lot of excess people, the tendency might be to train someone internally for a job they are not really suitable for. I am sure many companies still do this. Training and development make good sense, but the square peg in a round hole can be an issue."

Another issue that has been widely discussed is that, in the downsized, much flatter organizations that have taken shape, executives are finding themselves juggling up to twenty-five direct reports. Is it so? Yes, it is. However, most of our investigating consultants discovered that managers weren't having such a bad time of it as people might think. Comments Neumann International partner Tom Acuff, "Let's face it, the only possibility for a manager to have a team of twenty-five people reporting to him is where all twenty-five are fully trained, experienced, and capable of interfacing with one another and with other parties inside and outside of the organization: they don't interface with their direct superior manager nearly as much as in the old pyramid system."

Taking the point further, Buzan likens victims and survivors to "prisoner-of-war survivors, who all saw humor in adversity, all had a vision for getting out, escaping, making the best of it. All remained proactive. They were not necessarily the physically strongest, not the wealthiest, not the best trained or educated, but they had the mental muscle to get through it."

What this means in percentage terms of how many of us make the switch isn't clear, although a lot of people are managing the process just fine. What is certain is that there are going to be quite a few victims of this social earthquake and we have to accept that—look around and you'll see there already are.

Comments professor Cary Cooper of the University of Manchester in an article by David Smith in the U.K.'s *Sunday Times*, "We are entering the age of uncertainty when a great deal of work will be done on a freelance basis. I am deeply worried that people will not be able to cope with such a fundamental shift in the world of work."

The Haves and the Have-Nots

The shift to the new world of work, according to Linda Holbeche, "seems to be causing an increasing polarity between the haves and the have-nots—with the haves taking care of themselves and their futures with private health care and education and so on." Holbeche adds, "I suspect if this trend continues there is likely to be a gradual build-up of tension, resentment, and crime, similar to the trends in Europe before World War II."

MCE's John Doerr adds a perspective from the United States: "Unfortunately, the world may be dividing into the old colonial situation of the very wealthy and everyone else. Many people look at the success that the United States has had over the last decade in regaining profitability and competitiveness. On the one hand this has been very good—the country as a whole seems very successful. On the other hand, what is just starting to be examined is the social wrenching that has gone on as everyone struggles with the feeling of never being at ease. We are always worried about what happens next. Eventually this takes a toll on society and on the community supportiveness that I believe is essential for a strong society. As one computer company executive said to me, 'Work isn't fun anymore. I never have time for anything but work.' "

But it's not only the people who have to cope with this disloca-
tion to stay competitive; governments have to do something as well.
Says MCE's Doerr, "The question that society has to ask is What is
our obligation to these people? and What can we afford to provide?
In the United States we have decided on a social policy in which it
is OK to make millions cutting the jobs of thousands. The haves will
have more and the have-nots less. No one has voted on this, but we
seem to have accepted it as the way of the future." But, as Doerr
points out, things in Europe are just as bad for opposite reasons.
"Recently I asked a German manager from the former GDR about
his company's moves that reduced employment at his silicon wafer
plant from 8,500 to 356. 'What happened to the 8,000 you laid off?'
I asked. He said that most were still unemployed, but the state
was carrying them. How long can governments in Europe carry
the burden?"

Norwegian consultant and writer Arild Lillebo adds, "The European welfare states were built on good intentions, but the time has
now come to rethink the role of governments. They should concentrate on the vital tasks of infrastructure that can make our societies
run more smoothly and be more competitive, while at the same
time safeguarding those elements of society that should be pre-
served for the future. Doing certain tasks well is more important
than meddling with everything." Lillebo adds to that his concern for
less government in the United States. "A rethinking in the United
States may entail a greater government role in education, health
care, and transportation."

Brussels-based publishing entrepreneur David Starr adds his
concerns to that debate: "In the United States, I believe that the battle is just starting and will be complicated by parallel issues of racism, political militants, declines in land fertility, water shortages,
resurgent religious radicalism, and a declining middle class. I think
the United States is in serious trouble."

The Japanese—already afflicted with their own working world
dramas—don't see the freewheeling hire-and-fire traditions of the
United States as a solution to getting the workforce back on its feet
either. T.W. Kang, a Tokyo-based management consultant and former senior executive with microchip maker Intel, observes, "The
hollowing out of American industry is said to be around 25 percent,
the corresponding Japanese rate is still single digit. At a recent seminar in Tokyo there was strong disapproval of American-style hire-
and-fire policy, not to mention all the legal complications this has

REENGINEERING IT ISN'T

Everyone interviewed for this book (almost two hundred business professionals) agreed that the much touted reengineering of corporations has been at best a disaster, at worst cataclysmic—except for the very few who used it as originally designed—the key to a new working world.

What most people forgot was that reengineering didn't start out as a lonely, soon to be chilling, word. It had two others in front: business and process. Business process engineering (BPR), as explained in the megaselling books on the subject, was an opportunity to examine how you did things and do them better. Sure it might involve chopping staff, even whole departments and businesses, but this was to ensure the organization's future. Instead, scared top management read only half the recipe on the back of the box and reengineering became synonymous with downsizing. BPR lost its credibility in the mass layoffs that were wrought in its name. Instead of a recipe for change and renewal it was ultimately seen as the sword of doom, chopping without any semblance of creation or building for a new future.

Comments Mike Staunton, director of human resource programs at Management Centre Europe in Brussels, "It is quite clear that the majority of implementations of the reengineering process have been downsizing exercises. The original approach, suggested by people like Jim Champy of CSC Index (coauthor of the classic book on BPR, *Re-engineering the Corporation*), which is working with a blank sheet of paper and redesigning your organization the way you would like to see it, has not been the guiding principle. Indeed the move today toward transformation rather than reengineering process approaches is part of the recognition that you have to engage the hearts and minds of the people that work for you."

Dan Lund, who heads Mori de Mexico, a market consulting firm, likes reengineering even less. "There are interesting aspects of the reengineering literature, but the impact here is limited to downsizing without a creative counterpart. It has a bad name and I refuse to hear the word mentioned or see it used in any of our consulting work or documents. Whatever is good in the reengineering concept can best be repackaged with a less awkward and mechanical name."

The results of mass downsizing have been—and still are—disastrous. As *Management Today* reported, "Without exception, managers at all levels below the very top identify with their let-go colleagues and fear they will suffer the same fate. When you sack 50 percent of your staff the concept of employability provokes hoots of derision among the rest." The magazine went on to add, "A frightening discrepancy has opened up between rhetoric and reality. Below the chief executive and his cheerleading human resource department, a number of companies resemble nothing so much as buildings blasted by a neutron bomb." They could have added that the few dust-covered, jittery survivors are left in the wreckage doing their jobs and those of their former colleagues.

But there is another view, as postneutroned Bank of America's Jim Prouty points out: "I don't have a lot of sympathy for the stress levels of senior manager survivors of reengineered organizations. When we restructure and cut out the dead wood, we hope we've selected the strongest of the litter to carry the company forward. We're very careful about whom we select and have found in general that our people have thrived with flatter structures and more authority."

Great if the management is good enough to make it all work, but Erik Hoffmoen of the Institutt for Karriereutvikling in Oslo worries that Prouty's confident assessment of his organization doesn't ring true elsewhere. "Companies do not make a very conscious effort to deal with both the psychological and practical issues facing the remaining employees. As in many other situations, it is easy for management to assume—in the name of authority and leadership—that once the remaining employees have received news of downsizing from the managing director, they automatically—or at most in a day or two—turn in the required direction and get on with the job in blind trust. This reflects a certain arrogance, shortsightedness, and stupidity, that once management has made a decision the staff is assumed to have absorbed the news and motivated themselves for getting on with the job in no time."

Indeed, over the last few years, at management conferences and forums around the globe, chief executive after chief executive would get to their feet and like senators in a Roman arena announce—to applause from the audience—how many thousands of people they had removed that week, month, or year. No one bothered to ask the questions Why didn't you see the need to do this before? Why did you have all those people in the first place? Nor were too many of them discussing the fate of the survivors—those still fighting the fires inside the burning building.

Sally Haver of outplacement consultants the Ayers Group in New York notes that you have to deal with and help the survivors, not just let them get on with it. "The survivors are left in a company they think they know because new workplaces have been created out of old ones, so the feeling of familiarity and security can be illusory. If the cuts have been too deep—as is the case many times—the survivors are quickly burned out by the workload. This on top of their feelings of grief and loss over the departure of workplace friends is a real morale destroyer and must be promptly and effectively addressed by senior management, lest the company lose a significant percentage of its productivity."

Operations head of the international transport company Gosselin, Eddy Bonne, states his view: "Very few people actually know what reengineering is. Reengineering is admitting that you have been driving on the wrong side of the road, presuming you were headed in the right direction."

Art Ferguson, president of Mobil Petrochemicals International, who has seen major downsizing across the whole Mobil Corporation, admits, "Let's face it, many managers did a bad job and we hired too many people. There are whole lots of people in the middle you just don't need; the fact is did we ever really need them? What I think reengineering has done is forced a culture where you always stop and look."

> *Reengineering is admitting you were driving on the wrong side of the road with the assumption you were going in the right direction.*

"All the same," says Ferguson, "there is still a shortage of people who can make, sell, design, and build as opposed to those that measure, recommend, or plan." This statement highlights the classic difference between line and staff, which Ferguson sums up as "the watchers, watching the watchers, watching some poor bastard do something!"

Indeed, first-round cuts in some corporations were (if they hadn't brought so much individual misery) laughable. Staff departments saddled with the task of downsizing programs saved themselves; it was the doers—the salespeople, the production staff—that got whacked on the head with the downsizing sword first.

But, tucked away, hidden from the curious gaze of those who thought reengineering was a great game and a wonderful opportunity to blitz the corporate head count, there have been some corporations who have quietly gone ahead with the full works of BPR. Observes Gwen Ventris, director organization and resourcing with Syntegra, a subsidiary of British telecommunications giant BT, "Reengineering has been much abused as a term and disguises many far more simplistic management actions. Downsizing is a component of reengineering, but in my experience most British companies are unable or unwilling to deal with the significant issues that arise as a result of the reengineering proposition, since to be effective, it must fundamentally change the way management and the organization behave—do business. There are few companies in the United Kingdom that I know of that have successfully reengineered—Syntegra is one."

Peter Kraft, country manager for American Express in Hungary, says that his organization has also "truly gone through the reengineering exercise and the results are now being seen."

Blackhawk's European president, Jean-Paul Barthelme, also has had a positive experience. "We have done this ourselves and we have made no mistakes," he says. "Reengineering covers everything from downsizing departments to creating new ones, to both hiring and firing people."

It has been said that ideas acquired with ease are discarded with ease. In most cases reengineering has downsized itself out of existence and we are now waiting for the next quick-fix fad. The frightening thing today is the invention and quick rejection of so many often conflicting management fixes and their influence on those that purport to lead us. Despite a slew of evidence to the contrary, otherwise normal, sane men and women still believe that there is a Holy Grail, where the organizational answer is enshrined. Management seminars are packed with executives vainly looking for THE answer. Telling them there isn't one is not a profitable or desirable exercise.

come to entail. If we followed their example, whatever remains of order on the Japanese streets would be gone."

Another view, partly supporting the U.S. system but roundly condemning European overregulation and regimentation, is suggested by Tom McGuire, founder of Clarus, an international marketing communications organization based in Brussels: "To exaggerate what's happened in the new working world, the difference between the U.S. model and that of Europe is the contrast between capitalism and communism [note the small c's, please]. It's the gap between the free market and a command economy."

McGuire continues with two questions: "Why is the world's richest person an entrepreneur who built a software company in the United States from scratch in twenty-five years to dominate the global market for such products? Why are the world's most popular feature films coming from American filmmakers? The answer: the U.S. model encourages risk, commercial responsibility, and hard work. Western Europe has another breed of social contract—one that evolved after World War II—favoring state monopolies, highly regulated employment regimes, and oppressive personal and corporate tax climates. The social benefits in Europe may be more democratic (higher education, health care, and pensions) but costs associated with these benefits have stifled investment, risk taking, and entrepreneurism."

McGuire concludes, "The fact is that the specialist skills required to be successful in the new working world cannot be regulated by government. Private initiative and personal choice play greater roles in creating and sustaining those businesses that define and drive the new world order. Choice is the cornerstone of capitalism. Command is the hallmark of communism. Moving into the next millennium one system is thriving—the other is dead."

> *Don't expect government to provide the skills you need*
> *for the new working world.*

MCE's Doerr also addresses the U.S. issue from the "I'm really worried" point of view when he says, "In the past government and labor unions have played a role in smoothing out the rough edges of capitalism. Now we seem to have entered a stage in which the free market has run amuck. Unfortunately the tone in the United States is for less government and less willingness to work on compromise for the common good." Doerr suggests, "Don't look to the United States for the answer. We have taken the hire-and-fire philosophy to an extreme, and we are quickly creating a society of superstars and the rest.

"In Europe, years of overspending have left governments with no money to spend on further social programs. European governments cannot continue to have the overly restrictive work rules that discourage companies from growing and investing. Somewhere in between what the United States has done and what Europe has done lies the answer. Government has to be honest with the people as to the real choices or we will go through some turbulent social unrest as we move to this new world of work."

But for that to happen, two other groups have to be honest as well: politicians and business leaders. The former, let's face it, are unlikely to be truly honest, because there just aren't any votes to be had as a purveyor of bad news. Even local politicians are unlikely to say, "By the way, this town is headed for the scrap heap, so I suggest you pack your bags and leave; but before you go vote for me."

Business leaders are another cause for concern. So far their track record in honesty on a scale of one to ten is about minus five.

Hewitt/CBC, a leading compensation and benefits consultancy, conducted a survey across Europe for this book, and they found that companies were communicating better and communicating more. The bad news was the reason. "The news was so bad in some companies, it was impossible to hide it any more," they report.

Jean-Paul Barthelme, president Europe of Blackhawk, a world leader in the design and manufacture of collision repair equipment, speaks as a truly pragmatic business leader with a considerable degree of self-honesty when he points out that "honesty will be limited depending on the workforce you're dealing with. It is easy to be honest with a lean, nonunion-influenced workforce of twenty to fifty, but harder to be honest with a union-influenced, if not to say manipulated, workforce of one hundred or more." This may be a cynical, if accurate, appraisal. If more business heads would be that straightforward and plain-speaking in print, we might actually start believing each other.

Rebuilding Employee Morale

Mike Kami has no time in all this change for any sort of reflection on what's gone before. "The rebuilding of employee morale and loyalty is an essential task," he believes. "Don't try to re-create the past—it's gone! Slogans, pats on the back, and service pins are passé. Work on honest, mutual communication, establish sincere partnerships and relationships based on truth, not false promises."

> *Slogans, pats on the back, and service pins are passé;*
> *people need truth, not false promises.*

This view is amplified by Jim Prouty, a senior vice president of Bank of America: "It's much better to be up front and get the dirty work over quickly so that the organization isn't paralyzed by change. In our organization [which underwent considerable change] there is absolutely no incentive to mislead anyone on our business direction and performance. It's probably something to do with the American style of giving more rather than less information." Unfortunately, in many companies, the record shows that the

information was not always based on reality, or certainly not the reality that finally emerged.

Kami adds to that, "Treat employees as intelligent human beings,
not as sheep: easily led and misled. Don't promise job security and
follow it with massive new layoffs. Deal with employees as individuals, not as aggregate numbers. Above all, don't lie!"

But totally open and honest employers seem few and far between
out there in the real world, despite the best efforts of a proactive
few. U.S. consultant Robert Dilenschneider, who publishes data on
emerging trends, thinks that most managers are still far from dis-
playing openness and honesty with employees and worries that the
situation could still get worse: "There will be a continual search for
bad advice. Managers seeking an edge, or prodded to do so by others, will continue to toss aside decade-long relationships in search
of the Holy Grail. This is not new; there will be just more of it. They
gain short-term euphoria and an instant creative niche, but they
have to teach someone or a group all over again and rebuild an institutional memory."

Like others, Dilenschneider predicts "revolution in the workplace. Companies are using fewer, better-educated, and better-
trained employees. Compensation is increasingly based on
contribution and performance—not longevity and status. Restructuring has created a multitiered work society, with companies maintaining a small workforce for their core competencies and
outsourcing everything else." He adds gloomily, "Millions are already experiencing downward mobility and the end of the middle
class way of life."

Despite all we have been through and all we still have to face,
Dilenschneider, like many others, is, in the final analysis, optimistic:
"Sure, anger, uncertainty, and despair are part of the mix. But so too
are new ideas and ways of looking at life. Loyalty to business will
continue to erode and big business will even more likely be seen as
the bully, but communicating will change radically in tone, content,
and method as organizations reach out to stimulate change."

> *There is anger, uncertainty, and worry, but there are
> also new ideas and new ways of looking at life.*

Frankly assessing the present and what they have achieved in human terms, most employers have little choice but to begin building
consensus; in a downsized structure they have few options left. So

what kinds of changes are they going to stimulate? What's going to happen next? Can we stand any more of this excitement? One man who says he has the answer is California-based Bill Bridges, author of the best-selling *Job Shift*, a book that explains that what's really disappearing isn't a certain number of jobs or jobs in certain industries but the *job* itself. In an interview in *Personnel Journal*, Bridges explained that "the frustration is that employees are being told to do all sorts of things that fall outside their job descriptions. In other words, people are being held accountable for things that are part of the old job structure, but they are also being expected to do things that aren't part of the old job structure." The "de-jobbed world," as Bridges calls it, is "going to depend on how comfortable people are working in less defined, more fluid environments." As he says, "We have to get them used to dealing in permanent white water, and the way to do that is to put them in charge of their own career decisions."

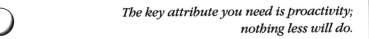

The key attribute you need is proactivity; nothing less will do.

So here we have it at last; the solution is simple—let's empower everyone to organize their lives the way they want to. As someone put it, "Think about it as You, Incorporated." The fact that many of us can't or won't make the switch doesn't matter. If you don't do something like this, you will be a victim statistic, because there is no other way, no cosy opt-out option, except to remain outside the ranks of the corporate roll call. Like a snake shedding its skin, we have to cast aside our old corporate suit and try on a new one. Hopefully, with a few tucks here and a few snips there and the odd stitch or two, we can have a new suit that we can learn to live with and even get to enjoy. But, let's look at this suggestion of Bill Bridges another way, the way Tony Buzan presented it earlier: "The survivors were not necessarily the physically strongest, not the wealthiest, not the best trained or educated, but they had the mental muscle to get through it."

There is the real key to our futures. It might help to have a thousand contacts, as we will see later; it might help to be in the right place at the right time; but the underlying attribute that you need is proactivity. And we are not just talking about software engineers here, not computer nerds who are going to start another Apple in their folks' garage. We are talking of cab drivers, who can diversify

their product to serve more than just people, of mom-and-pop operations who find a niche and market the hell out of it, and managers—yes, those too—who get kicked out of one job and find
another and learn to make the transition.

There Are Lots of Jobs Out There

Despite what business commentators like Charles
Handy, in *The Empty Raincoat,* and Bill Bridges, in *Job Shift,* predict of a stark world with no jobs as we know them, there seem to
be an awful lot of jobs out there still waiting to be done. Certainly,
at the blue-collar level there is already much more flexibility in
tasks, much more temporary and part-time work. In interviewing
outplacement and executive search specialists in both the United
States and Europe, it was clear that at middle management levels
and above:

- the job is alive and well, and recruitment advertising for jobs—
  especially management positions—is up over 25 percent and rising on both sides of the Atlantic.
- the head-hunting industry in the United States has grown by over
  a third every year for the last three years and—according to the
  Economist Intelligence Unit—is growing at more than 15 percent
  a year worldwide.
- companies are beginning to rehire, not for the same positions as
  before, but for new, more vital flexible positions that reflect new
  initiatives, new markets, and new products.

Additionally, according to Alan Schonberg, chairman and founder
of MRI, the largest staffing organization in the United States, the
middle management decimation theory just doesn't hold water.
Here's Schonberg's view of why not: "Of the 120 million in the labor force, 35 million are in the management or specialists areas.
This group has an unemployment rate of only 2.5 percent, which
means that the only people who don't get jobs are those that don't
want them." That of course is entirely within the United States; in
Europe the picture may well be, probably is, different.

True, some of these people are now working for organizations
that have outsourced business from other companies but they are

not temporary workers by any means. Schonberg estimates that "professional employment organizations that take on all human resource (HR) services and outsource them are now a US $30 billion a year industry; it didn't exist five years ago."

At a recent conference John Naisbitt, author of *Megatrends* and *Global Paradox*, stated, "Today, 50 percent of U.S. exports are created by companies with nineteen employees or fewer; this is also largely true for Germany, the world's number two exporter. Only 7 percent of U.S. exports are created by companies in the Fortune 500 and they account for only 10 percent of the U.S. economy. Unfortunately, much of what you read in the papers is about the Fortune 500 and they are often taken as people's perception of the economy."

Across the Atlantic in London, Andrew McGarrigle, advertising salesman with the *Guardian* and *Observer* newspapers, points out that the rate of growth of recruitment advertising for the private sector across the U.K. media has been 28 percent. Fastest-growing areas are public sector general management (where health boards, education boards, and town councils are seeking new executive bloodstock), which went up an astounding 75 percent over the 94/95 period. That is followed by private sector social services (the focus of major outsourcing initiatives), where jobs advertised increased by 52 percent. It is changes like this—some well reported, others less so—that are driving the new working world.

Changing the Manager's Mind-Set

The key must be to change people's mind-sets away from the past. Sadly that is often much easier said than done. Comments Staffan Kurten, a partner with outplacement firm HRM Partners in Finland, "People in Finland know there is a new reality. However, there is a big step from intellectually realizing something to accepting a change of attitude and behavior. Finland, as the other Scandinavian countries, has a tradition of social security. This also makes it difficult to reorientate to the new world where you have to take charge of your own life and career."

Fellow Scandinavian, Norwegian Arild Lillebo feels he has an answer for this: "You may have winners and you may have losers, but I believe that very few of the losers are really hopeless cases. Very many of those who are on the losing side today could come out on the winning side tomorrow. There are two keys to making this happen. One is to realize that people can be entrepreneurs in more ways than one: Bill Gates is not the typical entrepreneur. The other is to encourage people through small victories. Most people have the potential to grow and achieve a lot if their leaders let them."

Getting leaders to do just that is at the root of this problem of embracing a new way of working. Employees alone can't do it; the culture of the organization must support the changes that they have to make and make it as easy and palatable as possible.

This point is amplified by Erik Hoffmoen, a partner with the Institutt for Karriereutvikling in Norway: "Many people act as if they have signed away the distribution rights to their own product—themselves—on a lifelong contract. To rediscover their value and win back the obligation to take responsibility for their own marketing and product profitability they need to be carefully developed. Corporations need to make a conscious effort to redefine the psychological contract with their employees by redefining the balance between the company's and the individual's responsibility, and they can do this by organizing courses and seminars on the subject."

> *Too many people act like they have signed away*
> *rights to their own product—themselves.*
> *Don't let it happen to you.*

Hoffmoen adds the important point that it isn't just the individual who needs courage to change, it is the organization as well, for without that partnership these changes we have to make will be an unnecessarily long and painful process: "This will hopefully turn out to be a win-win situation, in that once mobilized, no corporation on earth can outperform the individual's ability to find out what is in their interest. When the courage is there from the company's side to take the individual's needs for their future career seriously, it will hopefully be clearer—and hopefully less traumatic—for both parties, whether the career is pursued inside the company or not."

It is this looking at things in the way they really are, looking at people the way they really are and accommodating their needs and hopes, that can make the difference, whether, as Hoffmoen says, they ultimately stay with the organization or not. Also, it should not be forgotten that we have to look out for ourselves, make up our own minds, not take what we hear as the profound wisdom. We should act on what we see and hear, not what we are told by others.

Back in 1970, Robert Townsend in his remarkable book *Up the Organization!* recounted this story: "When I became head of Avis I was assured that no one at headquarters was any good, and that my first job was to start recruiting a whole new team. Three years later, Harold Geneen, the president of ITT (which had just acquired Avis), after meeting everyone and listening to them in action for a day, said, 'I've never seen such depth of management; why I've already spotted three chief executive officers!' You guessed it. Same people. I'd brought in only two new people—a lawyer and an accountant."

Before we get too excited about all this opportunity just waiting for us to grab it to complete a happy ending, we have to remember that there are two things that will make a great deal of difference. Number one is where you are located: you are more likely to succeed in the middle of New York than the middle of Kansas. Second, if you have a network that you can fall back on, tap into, and use mercilessly, it will help considerably—in fact, it is almost an essential prerequisite.

> *Today's ideal executive: thirty to forty, well educated and experienced, flexible, assertive, motivated, open-minded, and a hard worker, willing to move anywhere.*

While there are those who claim that it's who you know, not what you know, that will get you on track and keep you there, it isn't just that. Points out Tony Buzan, "Let's face it, who you know is primarily based on what you know, and those you know won't recommend you unless they are damn sure you know something."

But before we go too far overboard about the career prospects of the new working world let's get one fact straight. Everyone may have options; some have a lot more than others. Frank Ebbinge and Lilian Margadant of Slooter & Partners in The Hague have drawn up an indentikit, a profile of their ideal candidate for outplacing into a new job: Between thirty and forty years old, well educated with a broad experience. Flexible, assertive, open-minded, highly motivated, hardworking, with no geographic limitations.

If you don't match up, don't worry. As we will explore in chapter 2, there are all sorts of new executive profiles in the redesigned corporation of today.

KEY POINTS

Note: Chapter 8 (at the back of the book) has a complete set of checklists to help you think through your future career plans. This summary is designed to help you begin to think about the issues raised in this chapter.

1. Jobs that have gone have gone forever and businesses that close aren't going to suddenly reappear: accept that change and become future oriented.

2. You will need more skills and need to know more than ever: think about how you can achieve that.

3. There will be few jobs for life: use this as a challenge to create a successful career plan.

4. It isn't the strongest, the most financially secure, or the best educated who will win in a future characterized by constant change, but those with a survival-oriented mind-set: consider how you can be like that.

5. Whatever people say—certainly at the executive level—there are a lot of jobs out there just waiting for people to fill them: make a habit of looking at job advertisements to see where your skills would fit in.

6. Companies need to have the courage to take the needs of an individual's career seriously (either inside or outside the company), creating employability. Is your organization doing that, and if not, can you get them to do so?

8. Too many people seem to have signed away their rights to their most precious position—themselves: make sure you own YOU and nobody else!

What You Should Do Now . . .

1. Sit down quietly (or put that plane, train, or bus ride to good use) and ask yourself this question: "What HONESTLY are my personal prospects for the future if I continue as I am?" Use the space below to write them down:

_____

_____

_____

_____

_____

_____

_____

_____

2. Now ask yourself the following question: "How can I ensure that in this new working world we are inheriting I can stay self-reliant and self-sufficient?" Use the space below to begin outlining some of your options, some of the things inside and outside your work life that make you a unique individual.

_____

_____

_____

_____

_____

_____

_____

_____

_____

Taking Hold of Your Own Destiny: Inside the Organization

Never cut what you can untie.   **—JOSEPH JOUBERT**

Change is the law of life. And those who look only to the past or present are certain to miss the future.

            —JOHN F. KENNEDY

So, if we all recognize that it's a pretty tough, rough world out there, how are we going to be certain we can take hold of our own destiny? Especially if we are one of the lucky ones inside an organization who have survived the wars and skirmishes, how can we ensure our future and success?

First thing to consider is that if we are still an organizational man or woman we are ahead of the game (getting other employment or going it alone are addressed in chapters 6 and 7). It has been suggested that what has happened to most corporations by now is like huge countries that have stood down their large armies that they don't need anymore. Foot soldiers have been replaced with new weapon technology, and our organizations, now in their broken-up business units, resemble small guerrilla fighting forces chasing down the terrorists—the competition—on their turf.

What a lot of people seem to forget, and certainly cannot see in the smoke and dust of downsizing that has still to settle, is that organizations really do need people inside them. They might not need as many, in some cases they might not need the same functions, but the oldest cry of a CEO is as valid today as it was fifty years ago—"I can't find enough good people."

So the key if you are inside the organization and plan to stick around is to make it known that you are there and that you have a lot of things going for you. The retiring type who hides his or her light under a bushel, or these days a stack of computer printout, is definitely going nowhere.

Stories that the so-called contract between employer and employee has been torn up forever may just be premature. Mobil Petrochemicals International president Art Ferguson certainly thinks so. "No longer a contract with the employee—well bullshit! You need the best ones you can get and once you train them you need them even more. I cultivate the good people around me. OK, you can get rid of what you don't need, that's fine, and if you want to use a lot of temps, that's fine too, but you need the loyal, mercenary core."

Ferguson's view is amply supported by Gwen Ventris, director organization and resourcing of Syntegra, a subsidiary of telecommunications giant BT. "I don't agree that the implied contract between senior employees and employer no longer exists," she says. "I do think that the company person is a thing of the past, but we believe that there are many opportunities to exploit senior management capability to mutual benefit."

"The company man is being replaced by the plastic man," thinks Don Bates, executive vice president of Sumner Rider, a New York-based public relations firm, "he or she who is flexible enough to survive almost any environment." And using a military analogy he adds, "Success in business will increasingly become the province of gunfighters. Maybe the idea of the Japanese Samurai isn't so far-fetched."

 Those raised with the new realities benefit from the freedoms of the new independence, not the fears.

All the same, others see it a little less cynically. Dan Lund of Mori de Mexico points out that in his country executives "typically carry their core staff with them throughout their career. It is not uncommon to find an executive secretary who has followed her boss through thirty years of ups and downs."

Management Centre Europe's Mike Staunton has a strong, new working worldview of the issue: "Older employees who have spent a lifetime building up employment capital with a firm are resentful. But, like with new technology, those who have been raised with the new realities have an advantage. They benefit from the freedoms that independence brings, rather than the fears of being responsible for your own development and learning and work life. It is a bit like becoming free of an institution like the army—or a government service."

But Staunton also identifies the big issue: "Trouble is that in any fundamental change there are many people left wallowing in the transition period between the worlds of the old and the new. That's where we are right now." However, you are not going to be able to wallow around for too long in this winners and losers world, not if you want to, absolutely have to, get a job. Says Lilian Margadant, account manager with outplacement firm Slooter & Partners in The Hague, "Redundant executives who are not prepared to give up their quality of life are going to have to think again or they will not have any quality of life anymore. People who get stuck dreaming of past glories are the losers of the future, and people who are prepared to look at a totally new future, using probably other talents they might have, are the survivors."

The American Way of Surviving

Referring to the differences between the U.S. and European way of looking after the workforce, notably a different attitude to social security and worker protection, Margadant goes on, "This is what I refer to as the American way of surviving: people use their considerable talents and flexibility in order to make a living for themselves and those that depend on them. In Europe people, on the other hand, are often trapped by social security systems, which although originally meant as a safety net have been turned by bureaucracy into prisonlike structures and prevent people from using their personal creativity, making them dependent instead of independent."

Neil Irons of compensation and benefit consultants Hewitt/CBC in Brussels agrees with Margadant: "Cushioning and hyperprotection are habits unfortunately deeply rooted in Europe with its generous and bankrupted social security. In the meantime it breeds dependency, and an individual's sense of initiative and autonomy can get slowly but surely eroded, while self-confidence gets stifled."

But there isn't a great deal of choice. People may get left behind, people in organizations may have difficulties in adapting to the change, but the train is about to leave the station and it might be wise to be on it, preferably with a first-class ticket in your fist. All the same there are strong signs that things are beginning to shift in the new working world's favor, and people left in organizations are getting the message that things have changed for good, that going back to the old ways just isn't going to happen. Richard Savage, human resources director of Spillers Petfoods, believes that "provided people see and understand the need for change and you fully explain it and explain it again and again, they can cope."

Adds Jim Prouty, senior vice president of Bank of America, "We have found that if you restructure correctly—that is, one big cut instead of several small ones—the healing process and the cynicism pass more quickly. This is all helped by the fact that there is usually more work for those that remain and less structure, making the job more stimulating, without burning out the resource."

Some places are doing better than just coping. In Princeton, New Jersey, Response Analysis, an employee-owned market consulting firm, is doing just fine. Says its chief executive, Jim Fouss, "I believe that an employee-owned company can produce more loyalty if employees and the company share the same goals and vision. I think that companies just have to be more open and honest with employees and this will help motivate the workforce."

The other course is that all of us left inside organizations have one specific target to keep in mind—think flexible. Just as *Job Shift* author Bill Bridges says, we must move our minds from the job description restrictions of a position—to break out of our organizational boxes—and become Don Bates' "plastic" manager, able to do more, able to reinvent ourselves.

 We have just one thing to concern ourselves with—
think FLEXIBLE.

Remember, if organizations invest heavily to train you, unless things get really bad they will have too much equity built up in you to see you go. So although one of today's trendy watchwords is employability, where the new contract between employer and employee is based on the employer's ability to keep you up to speed so you are employable on the outside when they don't need you, the reality may well be different. If you are a bright, technically competent individual, able to tackle different tasks at different times as the need arises, why hire someone else? Recruitment, as you hear HR managers moan constantly, costs money.

A special report in *Personnel Journal* points out that "progressive companies are providing tools and resources to help with career planning because they want to retain their talent. Employers need flexible, committed employees who understand the realities of today's workplace." So there is certainly a lot of life out there after the storms are over, definite signs of activity in the corporate jungle even if it is taking a lot longer to get right than most of us would have liked.

Here Comes the T-Form Manager

So if we now agree that the key is to be flexible, how does this translate into the functioning of the new working world's organization? Increasingly, consultants and management commentators are referring to the T-form of structure to describe what's actually happening and what corporations have in mind for us. And T-form executives are not those that wear T-shirts on dress-down Fridays!

Gunnila Masreliez-Steen, president of cultural consultancy the Kontura Group in Sweden, explains it this way: "Most large organizations today organize themselves in flattened structures as well as in matrix organizations with a stronger project side. Development usually takes place within the projects, so the role of the line manager gets broader and becomes an ever more complex role. So, not only does he or she need to be task oriented and relation oriented, he or she now needs to know change management and culture

---

OUTSOURCING THE PERIPHERALS

There have been a lot of stories in the Western press that start something like this: Imagine you are called into your boss's office and told that the organization is about to dump your department out on the street. In two weeks time everything you have worked for is going to be run by someone on the outside. They're outsourcing your work group. The good news though is that you can get on the list and bid for it. You can become an entrepreneur and run what you have done for years as a job, as a supplier.

Wow, pretty exciting huh? And this type of story is usually accompanied by a photo or illustration of a terribly clean-cut chap in a super suit and you just know he's going to beat out all the bad guys who are bidding for the contract! Not only that, but—although he has never worked outside the protective arms of his organization before—you just know he is going to make a huge success out of it. In fact he is going to grow this business; he's going to get contracts from others. Before you can say total quality management, he'll be riding around in a Mercedes. Nice picture. Sadly, it's totally inaccurate!

Companies don't give outsource contracts to ex-employees.

According to all the people we talked to, companies just don't give outsource contracts to ex-employees. Part of the reason seems to be that the whole point of getting rid of the department is to cut costs and change the personnel and improve efficiency. Those who have kept the accounts receivable or the distribution or the packaging or the factory canteen ticking over for years are usually totally unsuited to the role of external service provider.

So, when your organization embarks on an extensive outsourcing effort, don't expect this to provide an opportunity. It isn't likely to happen. On the other side, however, there are stories of entrepreneurial managers inside proposing to take their operation offshore and creating a business plan that they have been able to sell to the company. More likely these days are specialized outsource service firms who make unsolicited proposals in microniches where they are far superior to any in-house service on just about any criteria you care to use.

management. This organizational reality demands that line managers develop a T-form of their knowledge—both broad and deep—in the area they operate. I believe that a manager responsible for a large part of a flattened organization leads through clear messages on where, why, when, by whom, and on which criteria the results will be measured. They leave the how-tos to the well-educated subordinates. The manager will never be able to keep control over every step but certainly will control what is delivered, but without clear goals, good information, and a strong vision this will not be possible."

Linda Holbeche, director of research at Roffey Park Management Centre, supports that view: "The trend is already evident within companies, with line managers increasingly being called on to take

on HR, finance, training, and other responsibilities that have de-
volved to them."

In Japan, they've discovered the same T-form concept, reports
management writer and consultant T.W. Kang: "Even in the emerging environment that requires increasing degrees of specialization,
I believe the optimum profile of an individual to be T-shaped. The
vertical line in the T denotes deep specialization—this allows one
to add much value to one's customers and clients [even internal
customers]. The horizontal line in the T denotes broad understanding and lateral thinking, allowing one to put the vertical expertise in perspective." Kang adds, "The horizontal skills also act as
some protection in case the specialization one develops becomes
obsolete at some point in time." But Kang attaches one rider to this,
saying that we must not hoard those horizontal skills until they become unmanageable "in terms of functional tasks. One should not
seek to do everything alone or in one's own organization. In the
world of the new realities, there will be in turn plenty of services to
outsource to."

> *Success will be measured by how much you are*
> *concerned for the total consequence of the*
> *product or service you are involved with,*
> *not your part alone.*

U.K. management consultant Alf Chattell explains further: "The
only skill of value in the organizations of tomorrow will be the ability to make a difference—however big or small. The primary issue
will not be one of multitasking—that makes the issue sound like a
scheduling problem. Rather, making a contribution will depend on
more than technical and professional skills—although these are essential requirements. It will depend on people being complete,
well-rounded, and concerned for the totality and consequence of
things."

Putting us all in organizational boxes with individual labels on
them hasn't in the long run proved a very good idea, thinks Chattell: "As Buckminster Fuller pointed out, 'Specialization has bred
feelings of isolation, futility, and confusion in individuals. It has also
resulted in the individuals leaving responsibility for thinking and
social action to others.' "

So that's where we all went wrong—we managed in our command and control pyramids of the past to breed out the ability to

think beyond our personal job description. Now in the new working world we need that flexibility to see the whole picture. As Chattell comments, "The skills required to operate effectively in the new working world are designing, integrating, and creating. They are sensing and intuitive. For these essentially human attributes to find expression—and these attributes will be the only things in demand—they must be backed up by a wide range of professional and technical skills." Chattell concludes, "For anyone to have a place in . . . [the] future, the sole concern must be with the totality of what it takes to find the shortest route to customer value. This means understanding how to apply your skills effectively—with other people as required—within the context of what it takes to make a difference. People will be defined by the outcomes they can create or cocreate with others, not by their inputs."

Those inputs can of course change depending on where you are in your career and don't have to exclude those that are no longer in the first flush of youth but are still keen and enthusiastic. As Don Bates, of public relations firm Sumner Rider in New York, suggests, "Much of this change can and does apply to older people. However, since they are more tied to their ways, they have to emphasize survival skills over technical skills. They don't have much time for much beyond the basics of computers, so they should concentrate on bringing wisdom and intelligence to the job. They can work smarter than the younger executives."

Just as business schools have failed to replicate totally the managers they turn out—although in some cases they have had a darn good try—whether these T-form managers will have greater or lesser strengths in the horizontal or vertical plane as they develop depends on their different work experiences. But their commitment to the overall process, their lack of protectiveness, will be how you recognize them.

Not a Victim—An Opportunist

Linda Holbeche is certain that much of what we have to develop and inculcate in the workplace is a change of attitude, taking the negatives of worrying about change and turning them into positive new opportunities: "It really is down to whether an individual can come to terms with the new realities and accept that career development—and longer-term employment—is almost entirely the person's own responsibility. These may mean shifting from a sense of being a victim of a changing system to one where the changes represent opportunity. This more opportunistic and entrepreneurial frame of mind, where you see yourself as fundamentally self-employed even when you are employed by an organization, is likely to allow you to see opportunities others may miss."

Unfortunately, not all of us are that entrepreneurially inclined. However, the T-form management model seems able to offer at least part of what Holbeche is advocating. She explains, "Partly also, it is a question of being willing and able to push back the boundaries of the job and look for the chance to join teams and other cross-departmental functional project groups. This may give people a greater understanding of how their organization works and at the same time expose them to new skills and information."

If you are younger, you have the opportunities to learn the required skills as you go along. Start early at acquiring a broader range of skills than your parents assumed would get them through their working life, because you'll need every one of them. If you are older, accept that change is a constant part of our lives and you will just have to make the best of it.

Advises Glen Petersen of Lion Nathan, a major beverage producer headquartered in New Zealand, "I think with the current rate of change, people have to practice adapting to change in different parts of their lives. Those who seem to find a dramatic change the toughest are those who are cemented into a habitual way of living." He continues, "As it appears that change is inevitable, then the key challenge is to make it as comfortable as possible, even to the extent of finding pleasure in the process. The old adage of relying on the company is gone; people will need to become much more independent and take a greater level of ownership for their own lives."

 Look for the chance to join teams and other cross-departmental task forces.

That independence will come from acquiring and continuing to acquire a broad base of skills and knowledge. If we know that the format for the future (not forgetting that the future starts right now) is some magic mix of vertical and horizontal skills, what are these nontechnical, nonprofessional skills? Where do they come from? How do we get them?

Rob Kuijpers, chief executive officer Europe and Africa for DHL, the worldwide express organization, has this to say: "In order to be able to prepare for this new work reality, I would advise very active participation in project work, which is usually horizontal through an organization and therefore allows managers to be more fully involved in the various functional areas of a company's organization."

Make sure you can actually DO something, not just manage it.

Consultants Hewitt/CBC, part of the worldwide Hewitt Associates network, conducted a survey across Europe for this book and concluded that "appraising employees, managing the careers of subordinates and communication, communication, communication were the key skills we all need more and more of." Great, but a lot of these sound like managers responding as if by rote: "You ask this question, this is what I give you." There is more than a suspicion here that, if asked the same question twenty years ago, they would have listed the same three things. So, nice try, but we need a little more to go on than that. Turning to Gwen Ventris of Syntegra, we get a better set of those horizontal skills for managers of the future to have instantly at their command. "Syntegra has undergone fundamental change over the past five years [it has been truly and totally reengineered for a start]. To achieve this," she says, "one of the early areas of focus was the caliber and skill set of its management. From that, the characteristics we value and believe are important in the future are:

- specific business knowledge and experience
- people management skills
- ability to work in teams
- ability to work in ambiguity, significant complexity, and uncertainty
- ability to make effective decisions when there is no one right answer
- ability to solve problems and deliver results
- high levels of interpersonal skills, in particular persuasion and influencing skills."

Agrees Bill Ayers, president of the Ayers Group, a New York-based outplacement firm, "The companies that are hiring have been in the

MOVE OVER MICHAEL JORDAN,
GOOD-BYE STEFFI!

In recent years newspapers and business magazines have gleefully chronicled the goings-on of the fat-cat entrepreneurs, asset-strippers, investment bankers, and heads of major corporations as they have been getting paid astronomical sums for doing (on the surface at least) a less than spectacular job. For example, CEO *A* fires ten thousand people, watches the stock shoot up, and gets a multimillion-dollar bonus. CEO *B* resigns because the board sensibly wants him out. Again up goes the stock, and he walks out with a lousy track record but as a very rich man.

Although there have been a rash of CEOs cashing in on their luck—heads of the United Kingdom's newly privatized industries are the most blatant example in recent years—corporate compensation for the rest of us doesn't operate like that. Despite pay for performance (real performance this time), most of us are locked into some kind of salary band with those variables at best 30 percent of salary. Indeed in many parts of Europe taxation is so high and kicks in so early that rewarding high-performance managers has become a nightmare for compensation specialists.

> *Executive pay patterns aren't going to change that much . . . no mega sports star salaries are coming our way.*

Few experts see that our fairly predictable executive pay patterns are set to change very much. The notion that we can earn football star numbers in a short but glorious career just doesn't take hold. But there are a few people out there that see that the pressures on top performers to produce results will bring rich rewards. Says MCE's Mike Staunton (himself a former HR manager), "For the senior managers this process [big-time money] is already happening, but with specific strings attached. These can be things like a turnaround of a failing company where the reward is in the form of shares, which depend on an increase in share price. The idea is shared risk and return, and I see this as being a major change in the future."

Public relations professional Don Bates reacts to the concept of businesspeople getting paid like sports stars with this comment: "Business is not sports. In sports excellence is obvious, in business it isn't. You can be the boss's son and make millions, or you can just be lucky and be in the right place at the right time to collect more than your fair share of golden handshakes. Anyway, the most successful executives will simply find the companies that pay the most and make the best of it."

Xenia Kortoglou, managing director of the Athenian Market Research Centre in Greece, has some sensible advice: "I don't think that younger executives will be able to get huge sums for short periods like basketball players because one of the reasons companies hire young managers is because their salaries are comparatively lower. Also, I think it is dangerous to promote very young people to high-paying positions very quickly, no matter how competent they are. This practice only stimulates young people toward an ambition for easy achievement and affluence."

Neumann International partner in Vienna, Gerhard Krassnig, doesn't agree. "It is a fact that our working lives will be shorter," he suggests, "and executives will have to make the money in a shorter time frame. Also, I think it is likely that top performers will get huge sums of money for relatively short periods."

Fellow search consultant, Brussels-based Tom Acuff, concurs, but adds, "I think there will be a downward spiral on executive salaries in some cases and big increases in others. The result? A bigger spread between the haves and have-nots."

Bank of America's Jim Prouty's ideas fall somewhere in the middle. "I agree that we will need to make our money early, " he says, "because most people are out of this industry [banking] by fifty-five. Traders are already like baseball players—most are burned out by thirty-five."

So can we expect exciting, new compensation patterns, mega reward for a tough job well done? Not if we are still tied to the company store. Most big salaries and incomes will go to those who jump ship and join partnerships and entrepreneurial start-ups (assuming they succeed). For the immediate future it seems that compensation for the majority of risk-averse managers will be the same as before.

past few years decimating the ranks of middle management—the people who just manage people—so it is crucially important that our candidates market themselves as people who can lead, people who can function well as team players, and especially, people who can actually DO the work as opposed to just manage it. Again, the primary focus is on flexibility, openness to change, and tolerance for ambiguity in the workplace."

It's All about Renaissance

The manager that can DO something is what Management Centre Europe's Mike Staunton describes as a "change in the profile from being a one-dimensional to a renaissance manager." If this term "renaissance" sounds a little flowery, let's ask him to describe it better. "What I mean is that the manager needs to have an overview of the different business functions and a broad understanding of the external environment that managers, even ten years ago, used not to need."

For some—those recognized as well-rounded managers—many of these skills come naturally. There have always been executives who had more interpersonal skills than they knew what to do with; then there were, and still are, the others, who need to be well worked over if they are going to make it. But it is also—for those already smart enough to see it—a two-way street. Managers support the organization that supports them and vice versa; the organization likewise supports the executive.

> *Are you being asked to devise, defend, and develop your own training plan? If not, why not?*

For getting these skills that, quite frankly, aren't that much of a revolution, more an admission that some people were doing it right all along, companies that count on their people to continue to support them are leading the way. Across the United States and increasingly in Europe, organizations that care and have taken a less cavalier attitude to downsizing and really do want to build some consensus based on other things than fear are investing in their people (the people they want to stay) as never before. But one of the changes in all this has been the simple fact that often the so-called training department has been sidelined (in some cases it doesn't exist anymore inside the corporate framework anyway). With increasing frequency managers and key employees are being asked to devise, defend, and develop their own training program, their own career-linked plan. Rather like going to the gym, they can pick and choose what they want to work on, in the knowledge that it will make them mentally faster, fitter, and better able to cope with the changing environment around them.

And that environment has changed quickly indeed and is probably even now changing again as you read this. It will also do a lot for all of us to remember that there are a lot of young managers under thirty whose lives to date have been colored by change as a constant, not as an occasional visitor to the workplace. If you have grown up in an environment of organizational change, technical change, and pressure to embrace the new, it isn't as difficult to deal with. In fact it's life as normal. These built-in abilities already have and will continue to distinguish the new-wave executive from last year's model. Conforming to that T-form, the ability to lead multidisciplinary teams as well as to drop everything and pick up another assignment is going to be the favored feature, much in demand in whatever part of the globe you land on. As one senior executive greedily confided, "Show me ten of them now and I'll take them all."

Of course, we are not all cut out to be supermanagers, and human resource experts say there is a danger that the concentration is focused too much on the upper echelons of our organizations. Most of us will never get there. Most of us will be content if we can just make this new career structure work well for us, create its own semblance of security, and keep us employed for the span of our working life. Not for everyone the heady heights of top corporate jobs, and in the flatter organizations we see today there is less movement vertically anyway. No, what we want is a solid job that we can go to every day; a job we are proud to hold, proud to develop, and proud to share.

> *Not all managers are in glass-walled office towers;*
> *today's managers are everywhere.*

Interestingly enough there are still millions of jobs out there. And that is proved by talking to Alan Schonberg of MRI, America's leading corporation in what he refers to as the staffing industry. Schonberg's operation (with more than six hundred offices across the United States) is big indeed, but it means that it can handle assignments others can't. One of the assignments it has is to outplace many of the two hundred thousand or so men and women who come out of the U.S. Armed Forces each year. And according to Schonberg these young men and women (most are between twenty-two and twenty-eight) have the ideal profile of the person you want managing your pizza parlor, auto dealership, or small service business. His description of this group is an important pointer for those of us who don't see ourselves as the future captains or even the colonels of industry: "They can read and write, get up in the morning, are neat, tidy, and drug free. U.S. industry wants these people. Remember these are not college kids; these are the ideal store managers of today."

Schonberg's statement makes an important point that we are in danger of overlooking. The wonderful world of management isn't confined to those office towers in New York, London, Paris, Singapore, and Tokyo. In fact, it particularly isn't there anymore because that's where the hardest hits have come; that's where swathes of middle managers have vanished from the sidewalks and commuter trains. But managers (OK, often new managers) live on. As our so-

---

THE NEW EMPLOYMENT CONTRACT

We talk a lot about the tearing up of the old "come and work for me and I'll look after you"contract that supposedly existed between employer and employee, representing the notion that in return for your blind obedience the employer would give you a guarantee of a job and the strong probability of promotion and a pension at the end of your career. Now for many that notional contract is in tatters, ripped asunder by the dramatic changes that have swept through our organizational structures in the past decade. So what replaces it? Are there still the last shreds of a contract specifically geared to the hard-core inner circle you absolutely want to keep in the organization, or is there nothing to take its place?

Organizational consultant John Gilbert of Gillifant, a management consultancy company in the United Kingdom, says that the "old contract was formal, written, inflexible, and inefficient. The new contract is just the opposite and is ever changing. It is no longer," he suggests, "a piece of paper setting out the rules, but an opportunity for the contract holder to parallel his or her own personal development with that of the organization, for as long as they both shall last! Today's contract," Gilbert thinks, "provides time for thought, not just doing, and is an opportunity to improve by planning and prevention rather than the correction of mistakes."

Here's Gilbert's comparison of the contract of old with the one that matches our new working world.

The old employment contract:	*The new employment contract:*
• These are the hours of work.	• Bring your brain to work.
• This is the job description and here are the rules.	• Can you improve the way the job is done?
• We control our people.	• We respect our people.
• You have to do this.	• Do you want to do this?
• This is our hierarchical organization chart.	• These are our business processes and knowledge-led teams.
• This is your boss.	• This is your team leader.
• You work with these people.	• This is your team.
• This is where you will work.	• Do you know your customers?
• This is what the job pays.	• This is what the job pays.
• Your boss will tell-not-sell.	• Your leader will sell-not-tell.
• Here is some job security.	• Your job will change with time.
• You may get promoted.	• We have varied job opportunities.
• Mistakes will be punished severely, so be careful.	• Errors are opportunities for improvement.
• Be loyal to the organization and don't rock the boat.	• We will help broaden your skills and flexibility through training.
• Have a nice day, but not on company time.	• How can we improve your job satisfaction and enjoyment?
Do you want the job or not?	How can we work together?

ciety goes through fundamental changes as well, as service-related industry takes a bigger slice of the gross national product, so we need managers to run these new or expanding businesses. Also Schonberg is right when he points out that you don't need a college graduate for many of these assignments; you need someone well trained, disciplined, and enthusiastic.

So let us not forget that a manager is not just the person in some glass-walled corporate headquarters—managers are everywhere. By no means are all highfliers, but most do good, honest jobs excellently day after day after day. Having said that, back toward the top of the corporate hierarchy the search is still on for those elusive high performers. There is no doubt that the old top management cry "I have a shortage of good managers" is still ringing horribly true.

The Unconventional Manager Is In

So what sort of corporate animal are we in need of to-day? Enthuses Gwen Ventris, "We are no longer looking for conventional general managers but particular types of skills, wrapped up in specific, individual characteristics concerned with flexibility and adaptability, positive coping mechanisms, and chameleon-like qualities that enable a range of different responses to different circumstances." Support for this view comes from Don Bates: "Successful executives will be masters of dealing with the temporary. Those who want permanence in things on the job are looking for a time machine that will take them back into the past."

So that's it. If you are still inside the corporation, learn those multidisciplinary skills that will give you the edge over others, but don't forget to keep your professional specialization up to date as well. Flexibility and the ability to use that in ever changing ways will be rewarded; intransigence will not.

Now let's concern ourselves with another issue—jobs. As was stated in chapter 1, there is a view that jobs as we know them are going out of fashion. There is a feeling that we will all end up thrashing around in the same corporate fish pond, feeding on the same problems, dealing with the same issues. While there is certainly a trend to less precisely defined positions and breaking out of the organizational boxes is definitely a pattern, few of the people interviewed for this book saw total disappearance of the job as we know it. As we pointed out in the last chapter, the rise of recruitment advertising for specific jobs and the increase in head-hunting activity for specified positions means that although some may see the total demise of the job, it is going to be around for a while yet, at least in the executive and specialist levels.

Although some interviewees admitted that there was a coming trend where employees would have no defined positions but would take on tasks and responsibilities as required, the vast majority pooh-poohed that idea. States Gerard O'Shea, managing director of Dublin-based outplacement firm O'Shea Business Consultants, "I would feel that there are certain instances where this is happening, but in my opinion it is more a concept than a reality."

Norwegian outplacement professional Erik Hoffmoen concurs: "Whether this is a new reality to any extent seems doubtful." Felipe Uria of Arco Creade, a career consultancy in Madrid, adds, "This so-called trend is not being seen in Spain. Projects are certainly undertaken but tend to be added on to the day-to-day responsibilities of the employee."

However, there are instances where a knowledgeable manager can bring a lot to moving from project to project, and while it may never become second nature for all managers it should not be discounted. Remember, in this new, freewheeling work world anything can and should be tried. On this, Bank of America's Jim Prouty is more bullish than others. "We don't have a lot of people moving from project to project, but we do have some," he says. "My experience with this breed of person is quite positive. Usually the person has a very broad understanding of how the bank works, its products, and the political and cross-functional sensitivities. Where we use these people, the results are outstanding, as we could not expect an outsider or consultant to possess these skills; consultants are used for more objective and strategic issues."

What these people are admitting to, however, is that there is much more of a tendency for managers to be expected to take on other things, to be less than rigid in the makeup of the responsibilities and the work, to see the old departmental divides pulled away. Observes Dan Lund in Mexico City, "I cannot see a general trend here yet, as I think we are still the tail of the dog wagging with many different trends. Still, I do see the generalist being more attractive as a long-term hire than the specialist."

A Temporary Aberration

The other area of the new world of work that has, supposedly, been taking off like the proverbial rocket is temporary management assignments. However, it would appear from the experience of career specialists and human resource professionals that the rocket never left the launching pad.

First, it is important to realize one thing: we are talking management assignments here. There are plenty of indications that blue-collar temping is alive and well and providing a lot of people with a new, much-needed work environment. Second, it is important to get one's head around the concept and realize what it really is. Don't confuse temp management, which is permanent temporary employment through an agency, with a short-term contract between a company and a manager.

CIAO RAMBO!

Another thing that's changing in the bright new world of work is the CEO. The tough-talking, hard-nosed tyrant at the top is beginning to look more and more like a fossilized dinosaur. One of the reasons for this is that after a cold, dark corporate winter we are finally beginning to see the semblance of spring—and spring means growth. That in turn translates into a whole new set of skills needed to nurture and ultimately harvest that growth.

Andreas Durst, a business unit manager with AT&T Private Networks, explains it this way: "There are times, when frankly, you need butchers to kill a good part of your employees. But it is my conviction that people will not follow butchers over a long time period. Employees need a CEO with a clear vision and objectives in which they can believe. Employees need to feel that if they are doing well that they are well treated and appreciated. Butchers will never generate such feelings among their employees."

This suggests that in joining the new-look organizational track we should all be assessing our CEO to see if we have the right type of character in place at the top. If not, it might be time to go and find a job somewhere else that has a CEO with the right sort of attributes. All the same, you don't want to find yourself working for Mr. Always-a-Nice-Guy either. Top managers need to be tough when it's called for but able to use those carefully honed people skills as well. You get the best out of people who know they have a flinty-eyed leader if it comes to the crunch, who can if called upon hunker down and battle his or her way through. So choosing your CEO—not just allowing him or her to choose you—is also a part of this changed relationship in the working world. You should be privately assessing his or her abilities and future potential to lead the organization forward. Try it out on Monday. An honest look at your CEO—or even the whole top management team—might yield a few surprises!

Indeed two leading outplacement networks, European Career Partners and Career Counselors International in the United States, collectively estimate that temp management is not even 5 percent of executive employment.

From Dublin, Gerard O'Shea is certain there's little happening. "Temp/interim working as a career is not really established yet," he thinks, "although the concept of a shorter contract (one- or two-year assignments) is becoming more popular and indeed is relevant for the fifty-plus manager. There is a definite perceived difficulty with interim assignments both from the organization's and the individual's perspective: the organization is opening its doors at a senior level to an outsider who will not be a committed team member and the individual is still looking for the comfort of permanency!"

Staffan Kurten of HRM Partners, a career development organization in Helsinki, feels the same: "In Finland temp and interim working is not established for executives. In my opinion, we have a big discrepancy between how fast working life has been changing over the past five years and how fast—slowly in fact!—attitudes are changing." Kurten explains, "In 1989 more than 50 percent of all new jobs in Finland were permanent and full time; in 1993 the figure was only 28 percent. But this is a revolution that starts from the bottom of the pyramid; blue-collar workers have always lived with this uncertainty—white collars have not. So, attitudes toward temporary jobs, odd jobs, and projects have probably changed faster on lower levels than higher up the hierarchy."

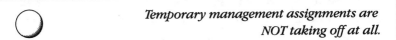

*Temporary management assignments are
NOT taking off at all.*

In Germany, there was a brief bonanza for interim managers when the former GDR had to transfer their economy to a Western standard, explains Herbert Muhlenhoff, managing director of Muhlenhoff & Partner in Dusseldorf, "but it isn't catching on any further. But then who promotes interim management and who needs it? Do companies cry out for interim managers or is it more or less the wishful thinking of some middle-aged managers (for some reason interim management is heavily associated with people whose careers have come to an end) who envisaged a meaningful activity by contributing their wide experience." And Muhlenhoff ends on a slightly mischievous note: "Occasionally, we get the impression that some head-hunting companies launch the idea of interim management just to try to create a segment that does not really exist."

Well, some headhunters might do things like that, but Vienna-based Gerhard Krassnig of Neumann International doesn't reckon there is much to temp management either, seeing it as "never more than 10 percent of the market," a view that American Express' Peter Kraft in Budapest fully agrees with.

On the basis of the evidence it would seem imprudent to try to build a career on short-term assignments with corporations. Possibly you could never learn enough or become integrated enough to become even remotely indispensable and thus have a chance of a repeat contract. So while temping may make sense, and obviously does, in nonmanagerial jobs, don't expect executives to be heading this way.

Then, There's the Gun for Hire

The other management animals identified by the media out there prowling the corporate jungle are the freelancers, the guns for hire, the instant, quick-fix experts. Do they have a place inside the organization or should they stay firmly just outside the organizational moat, giving those of us inside the ability to haul up the drawbridge and leave them stranded when we feel like it?

The upsides and downsides of becoming a freelance expert serving a broad range of clients is dealt with in chapter 7. The issue here is whether it makes viable sense for the corporation. Does what they can lose in control and possible confidentiality be traded off against cost and head-count flexibility?

My question to the experts was, "Do you see the day when, instead of today's employed executives, the majority are self-employed, working for a broad range of clients as freelance experts, as members of teams when required or as self-motivated, self-managed persons who pick up work like taxi drivers ply their trade?"

Management Centre Europe's John Doerr sensibly leapt onto the thorny issue of what is the corporation's and what belongs to the hired hand: "The struggle that the organization will have related to multiple people working for multiple companies is deciding what is the essential organization. If people can hire themselves out to the highest bidder, where does the corporate knowledge and essence live?" Doerr adds, "We have seen some companies try to solve this through outsourcing all but the essential capabilities of the organization; the hard part is deciding what is essential and what is not." In essence, he sees a situation that does not differ that much from yesterday: "There has always been a place for the multiskilled person serving the needs of many organizations—freelance copywriters and designers, for example—but we are now seeing engi-

---

WATCH OUT!

One part of the world where managers are overeager as well as totally devoted and enthusiastic about their work is Central and Eastern Europe (CEE). There, during the communist era, the practice of management in a planned, central economy was different from today. "We have watched their progress and the management process in the CEE develop since 1989," says Helmut Neumann, founder of the international human resource firm Neumann International in Vienna. "When democracy arrived and the transition to the free market economy began there were very few managers, but this has changed dramatically."

Neumann recounts how managers in countries like Hungary and the now Czech Republic had been forced to go home at four in the afternoon because ill-supplied plants were on part-time production. "So, these intelligent, communist-era managers educated themselves. They learned additional skills, they learned foreign languages."

Now with the added skills of Western management training these executives are turning into a race of supermanagers "as good or better than in the West, and they have to lock the factory gates on Sundays to keep them from getting to work!"

---

neers and computer analysts hiring out temporarily on major projects, then moving on to another."

Gwen Ventris says, "I believe there is a move in this direction, but I don't think it will go as far as you suggest. As with most trends within organizations there is always a tendency to move the pendulum in the opposite direction as a reaction to perceived failures. Most large organizations will demand a core of owned capability in areas that are concerned with mission-critical activity."

Perhaps the best way to leave this issue of the hired gun is to keep the option open to those who want to exploit it, either as eventual freelance providers or as in-house users of these services. There are countless people—most with a small three- or four-person infrastructure—providing vital services to major corporations (John Doerr defined some) all over the world. Interestingly enough, for many of these mini-organizations confidentiality is a critical issue. They know that their guarantee of employment year after year hinges on—indeed depends on—their ability not to discuss what they learn on the job outside the client's office. Like doctors, what they learn about the patient remains confidential. Often knowing more than many of the employees, freelancers can be and are useful assets if they are managed correctly.

Although the world of work has changed, there's a lot that hasn't totally disappeared; there are things recognizable from the past. There may be fewer middle managers than there were—although many of these have had new careers to develop and those that had a little tucked away or had a partner in full-time employment prob-ably did join that 5 percent statistic of temp workers. But for those still making a career inside the corporation the message is undeni-ably clear: you've got to keep moving, stay lean, mean, and full of new knowledge—just like the corporation you work for. Be flexible above all else; know your professional business as well as those soft, persuasive elements that help teams succeed and overcome their difficulties. Enthusiasm and the ability to produce, while con-stantly keeping a wary eye on your future, might be the bywords to follow. Remember, corporations still have a long way to go; many are still struggling. "Reengineering" may be a dirty and discredited word, but it doesn't make it any less dangerous. Employees that can look after number one while looking after their job and their peo-ple are the winners in this new world of work. Let's hope most of us can make and even enjoy the transition that's being demanded of us.

KEY POINTS

Note: Chapter 8 (at the back of the book) has a complete set of checklists to help you think through your future career plans. This summary is designed to help you begin to think about the issues raised in this chapter.

1. If you decide to stay in your organization, make sure they know just how good a manager you are, how hard you work, and how committed you are. Can you do that as an ongoing part of your work plan?

2. Younger executives benefit from a more flexible approach to work. They are brought up to break out of the constraints of organizational boxes: Are you able to do that?

3. Older executives should not despair—they bring wisdom and experience, working smarter rather than faster: if that applies to you, learn to emphasize those attributes.

4. The new way of work is to think of yourself as self-employed EVEN when you are employed by an organization: looking out for Number One is paramount.

5. What do employers REALLY want? The ability to:

   - contribute effective business knowledge and experience
   - manage people who work WITH rather than FOR the organization, using skills or persuasion and influence
   - work in teams as an equal OR as a leader
   - be that T-form manager: have intimate knowledge of your profession but with a broad range of interpersonal and other skills
   - work in ambiguity and uncertainty and make decisions in a climate where there is no right or wrong answer
   - in the end, solve problems and deliver results

6. You have to market yourself as someone who can lead people BUT function as a TEAM player and DO the work, NOT just manage it.

What You Should Do Now . . .

1. If you really want to stay where you are, ask yourself "What are the prospects? How long have I been in the job? Am I really enjoying it? Are my employers giving me opportunities to learn and prepare for the future?" Write in the space below all the positive and negative things that have happened to you in your work over the last six months, then take a few moments to consider them.

Positive experiences

_____

_____

_____

_____

_____

Negative experiences

_____

_____

_____

_____

_____

Conclusion

_____

_____

_____

_____

_____

2. Being honest, do you have those skills that today's employer is looking
   for? Write down the ones you think you have, the ones you don't have
   AND how you would go about getting them.

The skills and attributes I HAVE:

_____

_____

_____

_____

_____

The skills and attributes I DO NOT HAVE:

_____

_____

_____

_____

_____

Action items to improve MY skills and attributes:

_____

_____

_____

_____

_____

Timetable for Action

By the end of this WEEK I will have . . .

_____

_____

_____

_____

_____

By the end of this MONTH I will have . . .

_____

_____

_____

_____

_____

By the end of THREE MONTHS I will have . . .

_____

_____

_____

_____

_____

Getting It Together in the New Organizational Framework

Now the guy that got to the top, the CEO, would obviously be stupid to have a number two guy who was a lot smarter than he is. So, by definition, since he's a survivor and he's got to the top and he isn't that brilliant, his number two guy is always going to be a little worse than he is. So, as time goes by, it's anti-Darwinism—the survival of the unfittest.

—CARL ICAHN

You cannot manage men into battle. You manage things—you lead people.

—GRACE MURRAY HOPPER

Call it what you will, incentives are the only way to make people work harder.

—NIKITA KHRUSHCHEV

From the advice in chapter 2, we now have a better idea of the type of manager that it will take to be successful in our changed work environment. Mr. Bendy, the executive who can take all the punches thrown at him and still come out in the fourteenth round and deliver a crushing uppercut, may be taking things a little too far, but it isn't all that far from the truth. An ability to deliver value, to value teams, and take responsibility for your career destiny—even if that involves getting the company to pay to help you stay competitive—is going to be paramount. All that is going to take place within the context of a new organizational structure that is certainly less well defined and more complex—at least in the inner circles where senior managers prowl the corridors. All the organizational experts, that is, all those people who make a living propounding new theories of organizational renewal and direction, have but one word in their heads—"flat." It's an interesting word. First it's a four-letter word, which gives it the uniqueness of being incredibly short in an era where anything less than a ten-letter word, preferably added to another two or three ten-letter words, is required to be taken seriously. "Reengineering" had an unlucky thirteen letters! Let us hope that "flat" wins for its brevity and not its number of letters, usually associated with less polite words. Now what does this word "flat" really mean in the organizational context? "Mean" is another four-letter word that is still in vogue, usually tied to the other four-letter word "lean." When you put them all together you have a three four-letter word mantra for managing today: lean, mean, and flat. It may not rhyme after the first two words, but it is supposed to be what we are today, so never mind if it isn't catchy, long, or terribly profound—providing it works.

> *Three words describe the organization of today:*
> *"lean," "mean," AND "flat."*

We are lean because all the corporate fat of yesteryear has been sweated off in great globules through the "healthy" exercise of downsizing. Having learned our lesson, we have all resolved not to add to head count, except probably in our own department, where we are already conducting a pressure campaign with the CEO for some more staff! Although managers the world over would probably deny it, that is exactly what is going on—the war for more territory is back in full swing. Only the people, the tasks, and the jobs have changed.

We are mean because we are told this is good. Some companies misunderstand this word and equate mean with being tight, as in paying low salaries and getting more work out of people than is good for them. What mean is supposed to stand for today is tough. This can be accurately described as "If you come into our market we are going to kick you right back out again—just see if we don't."

Sadly, a lot of this can be ascribed to corporate posturing. Corporations like to think they are like that when in actuality they are worn out, broke, and fresh out of new ideas, much of the energy of the last few years having gone into how and who to fire. In truth, lots and lots of organizations are too battered and bruised to put up much of a fight; their demoralized troops don't have the stomach for more than the odd skirmish. Being cruel, they are also often only flat in parts, usually the lower echelons. Above there are often serried ranks of elderly majors, colonels, and generals who have by some organizational miracle hung on. As has been suggested, corporations are like a leaky tire—only flat at the bottom!

To be fair, here we are not describing industry leaders; we are talking of all those thousands of other companies that have been limping along forever and will probably continue to do so. Again let's drag ourselves back to reality and pause to remember that the advice in this book is coming from the smart set, those that do believe in quality and excellence and go further than handing out banners and T-shirts with "We're committed to quality" on them. However, there are a lot of others who don't follow this path—the sort that misread or were misled by that thirteen-letter word "re-engineering."

Our smart set from all around the globe seem to be pretty sure that being flat (not to forget lean and mean either) is the course we are all set on for the foreseeable future. This mutual agreement for the global body corporate to all hike off in the same direction does not, of course, preclude the fact that sometime, sooner or later, who can say when, we may well change direction and embrace a new universal management truth.

But for now flat is it. So let's take a few pages and examine, with the help of some of the world's experts, what a flat organization (the move to flatter structures is the phrase to use) really holds for us individuals who will have to try to survive and prosper inside.

Dan Lund of Mori de Mexico observes, "Our company is presently much flatter under my leadership than we were. We are at three levels and even as we grow I would see us maintaining three levels." But he warns, "However, the fewer number of levels brings democratic satisfactions and productivity advances only if the key

---

THE FLAT DISASTER FIRM

Dan Lund, who leads Mori de Mexico, recounts a story of the worst flat organization he ever experienced, one for which he worked. It only had one level! "It was a law firm I was part of in Los Angeles," he recalls. "We all did everything and were available for every level of task. It was a disaster, mainly because the whole thing was driven by ideology and not out of any practical dynamic to be more productive or creative."

leader is willing to provide an extraordinary effort. Let me warn you, flat is a lot of work on everyone's part. Not flat is easier, much easier, and is a lazy person's inevitable preference."

PR agency head Don Bates in New York points out that smallish consultancy firms make the best instant models for the flat organization as the "few top executives have to handle a multiplicity of tasks from planning to execution." Bates adds, "Contrary to what Peter Drucker has always advised, they have to both manage and do."

Indeed, in larger organizations it is a struggle to cut down those layers and layers of responsibility, command, and control even now with fewer people in the organization. "We've got seven layers," says Richard Savage, human resource director for industry giant Spillers Petfoods. "We'll have to see some fairly dramatic changes in capability to get below six."

Flat organizations only bring motivation and productivity if the leader makes a continuous major effort.

AT&T's Andreas Durst thinks that the flattest organization he has come across is "Digital Equipment in its sales organization. After a massive reduction of worldwide staff (from 130,000 to 65,000), between the CEO and a single account manager there are just four to five layers." Durst goes on, "I see this now happening in my own company and I think that this is workable in most sales organizations. In principle it should also be possible in administration and in logistics but it may be that R&D needs one or two layers more." Durst also says that you have to make sure that you have some real values in the organization that everyone can live by. Not just something to stick on the wall, but a document that lives and shows employees that the organization cares about their future as individuals (see box on page 56 titled "The Flat Disaster Firm").

Mark Nevers of Bristol Myers Squibb observes that "from a pharmaceutical sales representative" in his company "to the President Europe–Pharmaceuticals, there are just four levels." Nevers adds, "It is too early to tell whether this flat organization is working. It will necessitate extreme team leadership skills to be successful for the future."

Going along with the idea that smaller organizations naturally find it easier to be flat, Eddy Bonne of international transport company Gosselin admits, "My own organization is the flattest I know of. With around two hundred people we have a three-step hierarchy and some minor subdivisions in order to keep track of the various business areas we have gotten into."

Head of human resource programs at Management Centre Europe, Mike Staunton has three suggestions for his flattest organizations. "The flattest commercial organization I can think of," he says, "is Alan Sugar's Amstrad in the United Kingdom [a computer and electronic clone producer], which is two levels: the owner, Sugar, and all of the rest. The other is Richard Branson's Virgin Group, where he splits up businesses once they reach a certain size and communication gets difficult. This I suppose is a bit like the amoeba solution from nature." His other candidate is slightly different. "In practice, the old Catholic church model of five levels and no more would be interesting to examine."

Yes, it probably would. Once described as the world's largest multinational organization, the church's ability to run thousands of local branches and pass information through its truncated system—long before computers and modern telecommunications made it easy—might be a system to be envied.

One organization that has managed the great transition to a very flat organization is Syntegra, the British telecommunications giant BT's subsidiary. While much of that can be credited to a thorough and reportedly successful business process reengineering program that removed large parts of the formerly state-owned company, they are still an excellent example of the lean, mean, and flat variety that most aspire to. Says their director of organization and resourcing, Gwen Ventris, "Syntegra has just three levels of management. We introduced this approach, coupled with a series of significant changes to systems, processes, and behavioral requirements, three years ago. It not only works, but is much more effective in enabling the whole of the organization: accelerating the building of high levels of skill."

Jim Fouss, head of Response Analysis, an employee-owned market consulting firm in New Jersey, thinks that "as we are just entering a total quality management process, the employee empowerment we expect to release will enable us to build a flatter organization and go to four levels instead of five. I think that four levels are workable if employees receive training and understand their responsibilities."

Train and Explain

Certainly training would appear to be one of the keys to keeping this process going. Without explaining why it is happening, without giving employees the skills to deal and communicate effectively within these delayered organizations, none of us are going to get far. You cannot just take the organization and crunch it flat. Do that and you will squeeze whatever life it had right out of it. You must train the people—even the senior people—to understand that they are dealing with a totally new, hopefully powerful, but, in its initial stages, fragile way of working and managing.

"One of my clients has eighteen senior managers reporting to a vice president," says Brussels-based search consultant Tom Acuff of Neumann International. "The situation is not easy and training is most certainly required." But Acuff has concluded that "fewer layers are worth the effort, since it means much quicker communication, decision making, and reaction time. The real benefit is the increased speed in the company as a whole, not the savings in management costs."

Yvon Raak, president and director general of European Gas Turbines, headquartered in Belfort, France, doesn't feel that the number of layers of management are that critical because "according to

---

WHAT FUTURE FOR THE MEGA CORPORATION?

Deciding where and with whom you want to risk your career is a tougher proposition than in the old days before these huge changes came upon us. Some corporations are set to vanish, others to merge or be involved in takeovers, with subsequent head-count reductions. Already edgy commentators and those desperate to find something new and preferably cataclysmic to write about have been predicting the demise of the multinational giants. They are warning us that multinational corporations are now too big for their own good in a world where midsized companies are making the grade; they are being touted as not the place to go if you want long-term career prospects.

But there is little evidence to suggest that this is true. Corporate giants like Philips, IBM, and Digital have certainly shown thus far a keen ability to stay in business. Admittedly they have had to carry out major restructuring to do so, but all are set on a more or less even keel. What appears must happen in practically every case is that they will have to break themselves down voluntarily into smaller, more easily manageable business units. With that, they will have practically the same advantages as their medium-sized competitors.

For the individual looking to maximize a career, multinational companies can offer plenty of lateral and, more important, vertical career moves; cross-divisional and geographic opportunities; and considerable diversity. Equally, possibilities to be in on ground-breaking technologies and new ideas are endless; for one thing, they are often the only organizations that have the muscle to persuade the markets to provide capital for the massive funding required on some projects.

One casualty though seems almost inevitable—regional headquarters. These are already being affected as advanced telecommunication and increased centralization, often as a result of the creation of autonomous business units within the organization, make them less attractive. Then again, while Europe may see a net loss of U.S. multinationals with European headquarters and the United States see the same for European firms in America, the Asia Pacific region may well see a large gain of regional headquarters, as seems to be the general trend.

Advice for would-be large company executives is to find out as much as you can about future company plans and make sure you are part of them. Get into a growth area, not one that might suddenly be sold off or outsourced. Make sure you speak the language of the parent organization fluently; it will make a great deal of difference. Finally, try and get onto a project team that is on some ground-breaking mission or operating in a new field or region. Certainly you should have more opportunities for training and development, so if you ever decide to leave, those smaller, medium-sized companies will be on the doorstep with their checkbooks ready.

me a good organization is an organization with good upward and downward communication, no matter the number of hierarchical levels." And he observes, "Even if few hierarchical levels undoubtedly contribute to better communication, it is a good idea to make sure that only a few managers report direct to senior executives."

Roffey Park's director of research, Linda Holbeche, has spent some time looking at the issue of employees coming to terms with flattened organizations and she has concluded that "flatter structures work on the basis that employees are willing to adjust their expectations about career development." As she explains, "Traditional career ladders are disappearing and lateral growth is being encouraged."

What this means is that organizations have to help individual employees to be more responsible for themselves and for their personal growth. Helping them to manage that is an intrinsic part of the move to a flatter, more flexible way of work. Says Holbeche, "It seems unlikely that ad hoc attempts to improve morale by addressing only one aspect of career development will be effective in the long term. A range of organizational factors, which involve both HR and line staff, need to be addressed as part of a cohesive plan."

Holbeche believes that there are three ingredients to the success recipe: workforce planning, performance management, and career management. All three are vital to making the whole shift to flat structures work. Adds Holbeche, "A strategic and coordinated approach to redesigning the organization, ensuring that all processes, including reward and recognition, are aligned to the organization's direction is required. Research suggests that effective development and management of these processes is the best way to ensure that the organization has the skilled employees it needs as it moves forward into the next century and that those employees are motivated to give their best. Since it seems likely that flatter structures are part of a longer term trend rather than just a quickly passing management fad, companies who want to do more than just survive into the next millennium will be those who help employees take responsibility for their development and provide means for them to do this."

UK-based consultant Alf Chattell has another view that challenges managers to look beyond tomorrow and get a vision for the future. He says, "Growth and development will not be something that is done to people: human resource policies that work on the basis of helping people along can appear to imply to those being helped that growth is not the natural condition of healthy, well-adjusted people. Education, training, and development, if seen as necessary inputs for the individual to perform, can inadvertently enforce the corrosive view that the recipient is somehow inherently deficient and has little to offer in the raw state. Much traditional training reduces rather than increases the contribution the individual can make."

Chattell then describes what he believes are the organization's responsibilities to its people: "Tomorrow's organizations are primarily in the business of finding new challenges—not because this is

easy but because they will be profoundly people-oriented. If the
[right] mission of tomorrow's organization is to help shape a better
future for all, then it must uncover challenges. It is the tensions produced by challenge that fuel the natural desire people have for
growth and development. Traditional motivators encourage dependency and deprive the individual of the means of personal
transformation—the source of growth and creativity. In tomorrow's
organizations a legitimate motivator will be the admiration for the
unexpected things a person might be; the future requires the unexpected."

Greece-based Xenia Kortoglou of Athenian Market Research says
that she is "much in favor of a flat organization," but she believes
"it is most difficult to change an already existing situation: from
seven or eight levels to three or four. If this has to be done, it should
be done very carefully," she suggests, "not delegating to people who
cannot handle newly increased responsibilities if they have not
proved capable of doing so." Additionally Kortoglou counsels, "Before proceeding to such changes it is very important to consider any
psychological and emotional implications that these changes might
bring not only to those who appear to have been promoted but to
those who surround them."

Empowerment: Does It Work?

The two areas of empowerment and leadership are
causing great difficulty for many, particularly those who have not invested time and funds into training their employees to face up to
the new challenges of a flatter structure and are only realizing now
that this is something they have to do to ensure their future competitiveness. As one senior manager has said, "We empowered people we had no right to, we made leaders of managers without
teaching them how to lead." That, indeed, is the problem. Too many
organizations, faced with fewer people to do the job, make the sale,
and pamper the customer, thought that passing responsibility down
the line would solve a slew of difficulties at a stroke. In fact, it produced even more."

Outside of the corporate advertising that says Mr. Smartypants in
Malmo hired a whole jet plane on his own initiative to get a customer his delivery on time, it just isn't happening. Either that or ill-
trained employees are hiring lots and lots of planes. Most

employees are so hard pressed these days that they have difficulty going the extra inch for a customer, never mind the extra mile. Like quality circles, service, service, and more service just shriveled up and died with few exceptions. Let's face it, there is no way that a demoralized, recently downsized group of people—all doing the work of two others—can possibly give better service. It just isn't physically possible even if they wanted to. Consider this: if they do give you better service, they have to take it out on someone else. What we might well see is uneven service, where you get lucky one day and unlucky the next. In fact that's the sort of experience I imagine most of us have these days—a smiling airline cabin crew on Monday, a glowering set of turned-off, unhappy employees on Friday's return flight.

> *Passing responsibility to ill-trained, low-paid workers doesn't work!*

"Empowerment" is another word that has joined "reengineering" on the management fad failure heap. Few ever understood it; most thought it meant you could get low-level employees to do for less money what middle managers used to do. And this was taking place at a time when the other great fad was for better service to the customer.

In reality downsizing, empowerment, and improved customer service just don't mix. Companies have been playing lip service to better service, fooling themselves but not their customers. Ill-trained, poorly paid employees have taken the brunt of the stress and complaints. In addition, many organizations—especially those that had thoroughly downsized—thought, wrongly as it turned out, that increased automation and improved telecommunication would help.

Mobil's Art Ferguson says, "One of the things you owe your people after downsizing is not to carry any deadwood. Management is beholden to measure performance and contribution so that those who are not performing are replaced with those that can make a contribution." Suggesting that deadwood falls into two distinct categories, Ferguson says, "There are ne'er-do-wells who could do the job and don't, and then those who are sincere as hell but just don't have the skills. For those you find ways to help them or you stick with them through the outplacement process." But Ferguson holds to one key thing: "Remember, focus on the human element.

Even in a small organization you will have to manage people—you cannot just plug into cyberspace."

Ferguson is clear that anyone who "passed down responsibility because they thought they were saving money" will reap a sad reward. Richard Savage (with his seven organizational levels) concurs: "I am sure this is the biggest cause of failure. That is why we'll be cautious before we go further."

Anyone who has not installed a properly thought out training program to get these newly flattened hierarchies to interact with each other and take charge is in serious trouble. Gwen Ventris adds her experience that suggests that "I don't think that management can empower people by simply exposing them to responsibility and decision making and expect fundamental changes, without commensurate capability building." Empowerment is a complex subject that touches on individual capability, self-belief, confidence, and capacity to manage change. This latter component is most often missing in senior management and consequently affects their view of what is necessary at lower levels in the organization."

That's exactly what happened in a lot of companies: once again senior management forgot to read the instructions on the box. Instead they stuck in the batteries and pressed the "on" button. The end result was disasterville, with a big D. Confusion reigned as employees got it wrong with no middle management left to help guide them or train them fully.

 Even in a small organization you have to manage; you cannot just plug into cyberspace.

This is Dan Lund's advice to anyone out there contemplating the leap to empowerment: "I think that most people can be empowered up, if the necessary training and support is provided." And his next point is so telling that we suggest you cut this next bit out, or better still blow it up on your copy machine or document scanner:

> One doesn't set out to flatten an organization to see if it works. My sense is that one has to be convinced that the effort is a value in and of itself; then the risks of flattening the organization are greatly reduced.

Thank you, Dan Lund, for stating what most people have not seen as the obvious: one, you don't embark on this one Wednesday af-

FOR WOMEN THE STORY IS STILL NOT SETTLED

Although most modern-thinking managers would like to believe that gender does not come into organizational decision making, that men and women are judged as managers above all else, the truth is different. Despite all their efforts, women have just not made it into the executive ranks in the numbers that we confidently forecast a decade ago; at senior levels they are about as common as polar bears on the French Riviera. In truth, many doubt if they ever will, and there are already signs of hesitation by women to join the executive ranks. One indicator is the reduction in numbers of women signing up for business-related college programs in the United States, a sign that they may be shying away permanently from banging their heads on the glass ceiling and opting for other professions.

Headhunters and other consultants frankly declare that they are beginning to place women into senior management roles, but it is a tiny portion of the total yearly count. Asking search consultants from the Neumann International network provoked the response that the placement rate was less than 10 percent. In the former eastern European states, where the tradition of women in senior posts throughout the communist era has continued in the new market economies, it was around 15 to 20 percent.

Neumann International's founder, Helmut Neumann, who has championed the cause of female managers as equals in senior management and practices this in his oganization, believes that a lot of the problem still stems from the inherent differences in management style. "Our society and economy have been very much—still are—male driven. Now there are at last beginning to be changes, but we are still working in male-created structures and females just don't feel comfortable in them."

However, Neumann now believes that there is a "corrective force beginning to appear that may well change this male dominance of organizational systems and we will see new organizations structured on a female system." Neumann adds that in consulting and similar activities "women work well because it is not a profession structured solely out of male principles."

Neumann's beliefs are warmly welcomed and supported by Andreas Durst at AT&T, who says, "Women make their decisions following other criteria than men. Therefore, it would be very useful to have this additional dimension represented in management decisions. Sadly, I think at present women are still undervalued."

In the new world of work, the advice to would-be women executives is pick your place carefully, very carefully indeed. A lot of organizations pay lip-service to being equally open to male and female executives; in day-to-day, on-the-ground practice they are not. Do as Helmut Neumann suggests and find organizations that don't have a male-dominated culture built in with the bricks. Again that will mean doing some research, asking around, and building a picture of the kind of companies that might be the place you are looking for. However tempting, don't just take anything; plan your campaign carefully, get a lot of information, and, if you are at an interview, try to talk with some of the people you will work with before you sign up. If you are in a job right now and have some doubts, ask yourself honestly if this really is the place for you and are there any real prospects. If not, start looking around for someplace where your talents and ambitions can be better served.

ternoon at 3:15 when you have nothing else to do for the rest of the day; two, it is an intrinsic thing in and of itself and it must be treated that way.

Someone else who feels this way is Terry Smith, founder and president of Chi-Chi's International, a chain of Mexican dinner house restaurants that is rapidly spanning the globe. Smith's expansion throughout Europe, North Africa, the Middle East, and Asia is fueled by the concepts of training and self-reliance that lead to the right sort of empowerment, where management and employees know fully what their roles and responsibilities are and they are both trained and retrained to make certain it stays that way.

His advice to anyone in a company is direct: "Have a positive mind-set and spend mental energy looking forward and studying opportunities. Resist negative thought and avoid negative people. Be a team player and make sure everyone is winning."

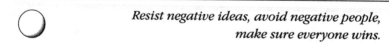

Resist negative ideas, avoid negative people,
make sure everyone wins.

Smith also addresses the issues of corporations large and small breaking down into groups and teams to get the job done. "In effect," he says, "the move to small companies and entrepreneurial enterprises forces small teams to accomplish tasks using a horizontal structure and multitask disciplines. This creates a learning environment for the team and requires excellent communication to maintain momentum. What is best about this, according to Smith, is that "people are learning together what is required to accomplish tasks and how to increase efficiencies."

Now we are beginning to see a real commonality of the proper purpose of our new organizational structures. It doesn't really matter one jot whether you are large, medium, or small—the same essential principles apply to all. Indeed, a small business is run the same way as a team in a larger business, well or badly depending on how much time and investment you have made in the members of the team.

> *If an employee fails to be fully empowered, it can only be management's fault.*

Terry Smith goes on to explain how the Chi-Chi's International team ensure they keep their working philosophy up to date: "We do this by putting our working philosophy on paper and then we all agree to the principles that would guide our work and our relationships [see box on page 69 titled "Philosophies and Values to Live By"]. We review these at a yearly conference to be sure that we are all still in agreement and to make any changes. All new team members must agree to our philosophy if they are to join us and they are held accountable by the team to the philosophy." That's another piece of good advice to cut out and keep handy.

In their roundup research of client corporations for this book, consultants Hewitt/CBC report that companies that have moved to implementing flatter structures have all emphasized the importance of communicating with employees and managers and making certain that training is in place. Companies are also urged to view the support that people need as an "ongoing responsibility, not just a requirement during the initial implementation period."

Hewitt/CBC also discovered two potential disaster areas that organizations and individuals involved in organizational delayering may want to keep in mind. First, you must identify your expectations for the program up front and make sure you match the design to the organization's needs; second, don't try the secondhand approach of importing a system that seems to work well for another company. The prechange work, tailored to company-specific needs, is vital. Hewitt/CBC conclude, "If a company finds that its flatter structure is not working, then it is very likely due to a lack of training and it should not have started the exercise in the first place. As the organization becomes flatter, managers need far more, not fewer, skills. To empower an employee who is not up to the mark and fails can only be the fault of management."

So, if you are a senior manager, think through carefully what you are doing. If you are an employee about to be cut loose to take charge and to make decisions, be sure you are equipped to do the tasks management has in mind. Ask for proper training and guidance.

Let's Hear It for Leadership

Further up our organizational tree, leaders have been getting bad press as well. Leadership was most succinctly summed up some years ago by management author Warren Bennis as "Managers are people who do things right and leaders are people who do the right thing." No one is sure if leadership is a skill or an art, but the 1990s have not been a good time for it.

We tend to put the mantle of leadership on the CEO alone. This seems wrong, especially in flatter organizations. What we really need are team leaders, project leaders, business unit leaders, who can take all those horizontal attributes and weave them together to form a coherent whole and lead, not manage, the people who are working for them. But again, like empowerment, this demands an investment and a willingness to make sure it happens. It requires organization, commitment, and a vision of what the organization is to become (an example of how leadership can be instilled across an organization is given in the box on page 59 titled "What Future for the Mega Corporation?").

The problem gets even more complicated if we bother to consider that a lot of so-called leaders aren't leaders at all. Comments Andreas Durst of AT&T, "One can learn the principles of leadership, but this alone makes no leaders. I believe a leader is born as a leader and has some specific qualities that can be identified and should be surveyed after the appointment to a specific job."

Jim Prouty of Bank of America thinks "giving leadership positions to the wrong people is management's blackest sin. The typical example—and this happens all the time—is to take the top-performing salesperson and make him or her the boss: he or she may have been great at sales but have no clue about managing."

PHILOSOPHIES AND VALUES TO LIVE BY

Far too often, corporate philosophies are literally not worth the paper they are written on. Lobbies, reception areas, employee handbooks, and front pages of corporate plans are littered with mission statements and the like that no one, from the chairman down, can remember a single word of. If you don't believe me, try it in your organization—and particularly in an organization you are thinking of joining. Most of these homilies are put in place because page one, paragraph one of the off-the-shelf, do-it-yourself planning manual said you must have a mission statement. The more expensive way is to get an organizational consultant to tell you that you need one and then spend a day with the top management group actually writing it. The result in most cases is a totally meaningless jumble of important-sounding, high-minded words that may describe something but certainly don't describe the business you are in.

As Terry Smith of Chi-Chi's International points out, a corporate mission or philosophy has to be a code you live by, something that makes sense to every employee, so as he says, "We are all held accountable by the other members of the team to the philosophy." And they keep it up to date and change it to meet the changed business situations they find themselves in.

Here's Chi-Chi's International's Partners Philosophy. See how much of this you could apply to the organization you work for or adapt to make it viable on a day-to-day basis. Remember, in Smith's organization every employee signs up for this. Does this sound like something your organization could or would do? If not, why not?

- Every partner will participate in the potential being created by their contribution. We are all partners in the building of Chi-Chi's International (CCI).
- All job assignments will focus on tasks that are action-oriented and require autonomy, entrepreneurship, and teamwork by the partners.
- All communication will be open and honest in every respect to every person in the CCI family. Integrity will be actionable.
- A positive team spirit will be maintained. One for all and all for one. Encourage your partner. All sacrifice and all profit. Together we practice team loyalty.
- Every decision will serve the interests of Chi-Chi's guests and CCI franchise owners.
- Growth is our primary objective. Growth of people, franchise owners, profits, restaurants, and guest counts.
- CCI is a service organization and strives to establish an exemplary standard of service by ensuring that the needs of franchise

owners and Chi-Chi's guests are rewarded for their loyalty with exceptional service. We care about service and strive to achieve superior standards of operation.

- CCI will actively encourage physical and mental fitness for partners, their families, and franchise owners.
- CCI and franchisees have a mutually beneficial relationship that is to be respected and defended.
- CCI is a business that sells intellectual property and communications. We will work to enhance the value by constantly striving to improve the Chi-Chi's concept, its execution, and its potential to expand in existing and new international markets. We will develop innovative approaches in order to introduce Chi-Chi's to new environments.

And the Chi-Chi's International mission statement is no flowery verse either. It states, quite simply, the brutal truth of why they are in business: "To create and be recognized by its peers as the largest and most successful international Mexican dinner house restaurant chain. CCI will build on its successful international start-up to become a leading casual theme restaurant in all countries where it does business and will capitalize on its image to brand the name Chi-Chi's as the dominant name in Mexican food. CCI will strive to develop aggressively in size through the use of franchising and company-owned restaurants."

Direct and clear, this statement is exactly what all of us would want our organization to have, something that you can actually read because it makes sense and describes what the whole organization should be striving for every single day.

Another service organization, but one a whole lot bigger, is American Express. Once deemed an overly aggressive organization—not to say arrogant in its dealings—Amex has come a long way in the last few years, making major organizational changes that have left it a well-managed, future-focused company. They have seven basic tenets of business they call Blue Box Values.

Their first value sets the scene for the rest.

- All our activities and decisions must be based on, and guided by, these values
- Placing the interests of clients and customers first
- A continuous quest for quality in everything we do
- Treating our people with respect and dignity
- Conduct that reflects the highest standards of integrity
- Teamwork—from the smallest unit to the enterprise as a whole
- Being good citizens in the communities in which we live and work

And those Blue Box Values conclude with the statement: "To the extent we act according to these values, we believe we will provide outstanding service to our clients and customers, earn a leadership position in our business, and provide a superior return to our shareholders."

Like Chi-Chi's International, American Express states exactly what it is trying to do and what the organizational focus (its day-to-day criteria for existence) is all about.

Those of us keen to stay with a corporation, perhaps because we see ourselves fitting well into the renaissance manager mold, would do well to check out at the first opportunity what the mission statement and the philosophy of the company we work for really are. Moreover, ask people if they know what the mission of the company is; just hope someone can find a copy.

When you do find the mission statement, take a good, long, hard look at it. Does it simply state the case, or does it look like it was put together by a committee of camels pretending to be leaders. Every business needs a focus, and a focus that is able to change and adapt. Just as Ricardo Semler points out that leaders are situational, so too should the values by which an organization lives be situational.

Neil Irons of Hewitt/CBC believes that it is only the organizations that can create a "working environment that will give people the opportunity to express their own values and recognize similar values in others that will be truly successful tomorrow. That's where you will get the enthusiastic, motivated, and high-performing individuals gathered around a shared vision, a mission not only stated but also alive."

Irons concludes, "Ask your people what their values are and forge a meaningful mission statement that genuinely reflects what they expressed. Then don't bury it in a drawer or put it in a nice frame. Recall it; bring it to life by believing in it yourself like Gepetto and his Pinocchio."

Prouty makes a specific comment about bad management that makes assumptions that people can just get on with a new role without any proper training or preparation: "You cannot take your top performer and assume he or she can use the same skills that made him or her a top performer to become a top manager."

Durst adds to his earlier thoughts and continues, "Too many senior executives are not leaders themselves. Consequently, they do not know how to identify a person with the talent to lead. Therefore, too many politicians and bluffers are appointed in strategic positions, where they focus on their own job protection, instead of on business success." Honestly, Durst admits, "Of course this happens in most organizations, also in mine."

We should all—at least all of us who expect that we are going to get something useful and long term out of our commitment to the new organization—remember one thing. The contract has changed. We are no longer there at the behest of top management; the contract must be a two-way street. So what we need to ask ourselves is "Just who is flying the organizational plane? What are they really like? Are they actually any damn good? Are they headed straight for a large, looming mountain? If so, is it time I got out of here?" Good advice is be honest with yourself and don't wait for the crash; there are always dead and wounded all over the place. Sneak to the door, grab a parachute, and jump!

> *You cannot take a top performer and assume the same skills will make him or her a top manager.*

Having said that, many heads of business are trying hard in the extreme to make leadership work. President Europe of Blackhawk, a world leader in the design and manufacture of collision repair equipment, Jean-Paul Barthelme, has fostered much more of a leadership culture out of survival necessity as much as anything else. He reports that "in our organization, managers have to be leaders above all else and you have to give these leaders the right working environment, responsibilities, and authority to put this leadership into practice." Barthelme admits, "Yes, I do think in many organizations they got it wrong. In our case we have an organization that was forced by the competitive and economic environment to become lean and mean. To do this, you will only survive with a management leadership approach." Would that others would heed this advice and make the changes necessary for peak performance.

To add to this debate, Don Bates in New York has a thought to share: "A lot of people in business say their company's success is everyone's responsibility, but if it's everyone's responsibility then it's no one's responsibility. People should think responsibly on the job, but their role should be tasked accordingly—too many cooks spoil the soup."

Maverick Brazilian management commentator Ricardo Semler— most famous for empowering his workforce to the point where they choose their own leaders by voting for them every six months—thinks much of our attitude to leadership is totally confused because we have been taught to think about leadership the wrong way, and no one has bothered to challenge this muddled-headed thinking.

Scolds Semler, "Most of us will eventually come to the conclusion that the right leader for a given situation is not the right leader for another one—so how come we hire people for two, three, five, eight years at a time in the same job? How many times has the situation changed and we haven't changed the person? In a workshop I do, I ask five or six people to come up on the stage and imagine they are in a situation where they're all in a plane that has just crashed in the Alps. You're in trouble, the rest of the people have died, and you're the pilot, so please do something. Then the people start talking to one another and in about four or five minutes you have a new leader. It's rarely the pilot, because you have a one in six chance you chose the right leader for them. Now you take the same group fifteen minutes later and say, 'Let's consider another situation. Let's assume you're an environmental group and you know that this afternoon a chemical company is going to dump waste in the river, so please do something.' And in a couple of minutes you have a new leader. It's never the same one." Semler goes on, "Now, if we accept that leadership is situational how can we possibly be making choices the way we do except if we have created organizations that are petrified so that they will only make marginal changes."

In Semler's case what he did with his organization was revolutionary, taking empowerment and the role of leaders to a new dimension. A strategy possibly too rich for the blood of many organizations to even attempt it, Semler and his employees—and there are a lot of them—make it work, day after day, week after week, month after month, and year after year—a true-life case of leadership and empowerment working in synergy.

"We told people, 'Look, we don't care about how you dress, when you come to work, what your title is. The first thing we want you to do is come to work anytime you want, because every six months the business unit you're in (fifty or one hundred people) will put together a list of all the people they think they need and hopefully you will be on that list.' Now the thing is they can lobby their friends to get on that list, they can do anything they like, but if you show up every day at eleven o'clock and you leave at one o'clock but you sell a hell of a lot you're going to be on the list. If you come in at the right time and stay the whole day and you're not productive, you're not going to be on the list. So what we have said is that we have no time for boring school rules. So we don't care how you dress, because if you visit IBM in tennis shoes and shorts you're probably not going to sell very much, and if you don't sell much, you're not going to be on that list. Now if you wear a dark suit and a white shirt and you also don't sell very much, you're not going to be on the list either."

Wouldn't it be great if companies could free up their collective corporate heads and learn to think like that? Not only would business life be exciting but we might also accomplish a lot more with a greater feeling of satisfaction. The question we should all ask ourselves in the light of that story is "Would I be on that list?"

For those of us who have chosen to stay in the business sphere, especially those of us who aspire to a more senior management role, we have got to find ways to free ourselves—and convince others to go along with the plan—from a lot of the conventional baggage we are carrying around with us. As so many business watchers will testify, managers are still protecting their turf; the medieval

---

LEARNING FOR LEADERSHIP

Lion Nathan is one of New Zealand's leading corporations. It is an internationally minded company that has been on a long-term acquisition and market development trail throughout the Asia Pacific region. Lion Nathan has developed a leadership practice model that can be a useful guide for others. Part of the company's overall development process, the model has been a powerful tool in getting leadership to the people who need it in flatter organizations, those that have the responsibility for team leadership. This is the kind of investment that organizations who will be successful in the future have to make in their people today.

This is how it works:

Managers are given specific feedback from their subordinates . . .

- They assess themselves against thirty-six leadership qualities
- They are then assessed by six subordinates
- Results are given independently
- We then conduct a three-day program on improving skills

See Tables 3–1 through 3–3.

TABLE 3–1

The 36 Leadership Qualities

Developing and Communicating a Strategic Vision	Leading a Long-Term Commitment to Executional Excellence	Demonstrating a Responsive Leadership Style	Creating a Climate of Individual Responsibility	Providing Feedback and Coaching for Results	Demonstrating High Levels of Integrity and Honesty
1. Staying abreast of changing industry and market conditions.	7. Establishing high performance goals and standards for direct reports.	12. Demonstrating a sense of urgency in your leadership style.	18. Giving direct reports the opportunity to provide input into individual goals.	24. Being supportive and helpful in contacts with direct reports.	31. Behaving in a way that demonstrates and communicates high integrity.
2. Maintaining an understanding of competitors' strengths and weaknesses.	8. Operating as player/coach by demonstrating hands-on executional excellence.	13. Dealing effectively with multiple priorities and conflicting issues.	19. Being clear and thorough in delegating responsibilities.	25. Going to bat for direct reports when you feel they are right.	32. Being direct and candid in dealing with people.
3. Understanding the critical leverage points of the business.	9. Selecting and retaining the best people for the organization.	14. Encouraging new ideas and alternative points of view.	20. Expecting direct reports to find and correct their own errors rather than doing this for them.	26. Recognizing direct reports for good performance more than criticizing shortcomings.	33. Balancing achievement of short-term gains against the long-term vision for the business.
4. Helping direct reports understand the company's business and objectives.	10. Working constructively with direct reports to improve their executional excellence.	15. Managing change in a thoughtful and well-planned, rather than a reactive, manner.	21. Encouraging innovation and calculating risk-taking.	27. Encouraging people to greater levels of performance.	34. Demonstrating a set of personal values based on honesty, consistency, feedback, and trust.
5. Developing goals and objectives that reflect the long-term needs of the business.	11. Relating rewards to results and executional excellence rather than to other factors such as seniority or personal relationships.	16. Confronting conflict situations in an honest and direct manner.	22. Encouraging people to stay close to the customer through leading by example.	28. Providing ongoing feedback on career development.	35. Being willing to speak out on issues even when your view isn't popular.
6. Communicating an exciting vision of the future for the business.		17. Giving direct reports a clear-cut decision when they need one.	23. Rewarding people for trying new things rather than punishing them for mistakes.	29. Providing feedback that is even-handed and fair.	36. Demonstrating a balance between individual and team—being a good team player.
				30. Regularly coaching direct reports on how to succeed within the company.	

TABLE 3–2
Lion Nathan Team Leadership Practices

I. Understanding Others	II. Driving Toward Results	III. Making a Contribution
1. Listening carefully to what others have to say.	7. Keeping people focused on what the team is trying to accomplish.	12. Being willing to share the resources under your control.
2. Giving credit to or sharing credit with others.	8. Focusing on issues rather than personalities.	13. Adding real value to tasks and projects versus not making a meaningful contribution.
3. Seeking others' contributions when working on projects, tasks, etc.	9. Openly confronting problems and different points of view.	14. Being a person who delivers what is promised.
4. Avoiding being overconcerned about one's own turf.	10. Actively seeking mutually acceptable solutions.	15. Seeking win/win solutions to conflicts.
5. Understanding the agendas of other members of the team.	11. Helping the team work effectively together.	16. Not giving up your position on an issue too easily.
6. Without emotion, resolving conflict.		

TABLE 3–3
Human Resource Assessment

I. An Effective Business Partner	x	II. An Outstanding Functional Resource	=	III. An Influential Change Agent
1. Having a solid understanding of the goals and objectives of the business		8. Being knowledgeable about HR policies, procedures, and systems.		16. Adapting quickly to changing business conditions.
2. Understanding business strategies and directions.		9. Demonstrating a high level of skill in recruiting, development, performance appraisal, rewards, and organizational design.		17. Anticipating problems and opportunities facing managers.
3. Understanding the profit dynamics of the business.				18. Developing good working relationships with other members of the business team.
4. Demonstrating a breadth of understanding across other functions.		10. Providing quality, common sense advice and counsel on human resource matters.		19. Encouraging an open airing of differences and disagreements.
5. Being actively involved in the business planning process.		11. Keeping abreast of new developments in the human resource field.		20. Effectively working out conflicts with people.
6. Developing human resource plans that are clearly driven by business strategies.		12. Proactively understanding legal/ regulatory issues that impact the business.		21. Communicating views openly, honestly, and directly.
7. Understanding and communicating how human resource actions impact the business.		13. Efficiently managing HR administrative matters.		22. Behaving in a way that leads others to trust you.
		14. Keeping personal commitments and following up.		23. Demonstrating personal values in a consistent way.
		15. Consistently emphasizing the company's statement of purpose and fundamental principles.		

baron tendency is still there despite the huge shocks of change that have been rattling the organizational windows and buckling much of the framework. Frankly, too many executives have not learned enough from these lessons that they should see all around them. Companies that expect to succeed in the future must make people investment a paramount goal. They must realize, long term, they can only get out what they put in.

As Bill Ayers, president of the Ayers Group in New York, and his vice president Sally Haver observe, "These are the sort of characteristics you need to look for in choosing a particular company to work with:

- Companies that invest in their people, to keep skill-sets current
- Companies that have gone to performance-based compensation models, that reward what the person has delivered over the past year versus seniority or other criteria
- Companies that go to broadbanding [a term used when many traditional salary grades are collapsed into a few wide *bands* for purposes of managing career growth and administering pay, an essential part of a flat structure reward process] and lateral moves when vertical movement is difficult or precluded. This helps valued employees learn new skills, keeps them from getting stale, and gives them a sense of movement within the company.
- Companies that keep an ever vigilant eye on their marketplace, their competitors, and new developments in their field; companies that try to stay ahead of the curve
- Companies that are willing to try new configurations to make things work better: reengineering efforts for example that might replace hierarchical structures with project teams that disband at the end of the project and that have members that can switch roles from leader to team member."

Watch out for yourself . . . don't get stuck in the wrong company with the wrong attitude in the wrong industry.

What Ayers and Haver are saying is "Stay aware and measure your organization weekly. Don't get stuck in the wrong job in the wrong company, with the wrong attitude in the wrong industry."

We must all ask ourselves what we want. What is our career path? If we find ourselves stuck in an irresponsible organization that won't invest in the future (and that means our personal futures), then we must move somewhere with better prospects. Moving may be difficult and traumatic in the short term, but it will pay off later.

What the message says is that today we alone control our own careers. We must do that in a way that ensures, no matter how bad the organization's management may be, that we can manage our own development and future with confidence.

In Search of an Excellent Place to Work

In Search of Excellence by Thomas J. Peters and Robert H. Waterman, Jr. was a best-selling book. It should now be a motto for all of us in terms of the places we want to work. Asking a group of managers what they see as excellent places to work provokes a variety of responses, but to give some idea of the types of corporation you might want to consider, here are the top ones distilled from the observations of some of the experts contributing to this book. Note how many companies get repeat praise. Obviously there are many more. I have picked only the most international examples, and these are a good guide to the kind of criteria you should apply to your ideal company, wherever you are and whatever business you want to be in.

- Jim Fouss (Response Analysis, Princeton, New Jersey): Microsoft, ruthless in the marketplace. Citibank, innovative. Motorola, well managed. Fidelity Investments, both consumer oriented and innovative.
- Carlos Cortes (Neumann International, Madrid): El Corte Ingles (Spanish department store chain), excellent management and commitment to people development. Asea Brown Boveri (ABB), investment in international people development. Banco Santander, excellent management.
- Lilian Margadant (Slooter & Partners, The Hague): Ahold (supermarket chain), consistent in their refusal to make any mistakes, excellent people development. Heineken, strong positioning and excellent results.
- Gwen Ventris (Syntegra, London): Microsoft, for its domination of the marketplace. Hanson Industries, for its financial strength,

ruthless focus, and honesty (it doesn't pretend to be anything else). The Body Shop, for its integrity, ecological stance, and marketing. Benetton, for its innovation, warehousing, use of IT, and management of subcontractors.

- Daniel Grenon (Neumann International, Paris): ABB, excellent entrepreneurial culture and organization. Hewlett Packard, very good organizationally and people oriented. Gillette, innovative and retains good people. LVMH (French luxury goods maker), excellent management and seeks to recruit very best talent.
- Jim Prouty (Bank of America, Frankfurt): Citibank, a truly global organization with a vision of the consumer and financial markets of the future. Big risk-takers and ruthless. Morgan, the "J" and "P" stand for "Just Perfect"; an organization that really believes in quality: quality people, quality clients, quality earnings—there is no match in the banking field. Microsoft, brains, innovation, and a wild-frontier approach to a wild frontier. American Airlines, very tough management, trailblazers in their industry, and survivors in a very difficult business.
- Tom Acuff (Neumann International, Brussels): AT&T, management going in the right direction. Environmental Resources Management (ERM), flat organization and excellent people. Sylvania Lighting International, smallest, most proactive of the big four lighting companies, with a top management that are agents of change. Bombardier, exceptional commitment to people development, noncompromising on quality of people hired.
- Peter Kraft (American Express, Budapest): General Electric, for their fantastic financial track record. Federal Express, for fantastic customer service orientation. Internationale Nederlanden Bank (INGBank), aggressive customer service orientation, especially in central and eastern Europe. ABB, for their technical achievements and financial orientation.
- Gerhard Krassnig (Neumann International, Vienna): Hewlett Packard, commitment to people development. IBM, excellent management. SAP, a major player in the software business headquartered in Munich, Germany, very realistic and conservative business strategy. BMW, ability to reorganize and reengineer the organization as well as excellent products. McDonald's, perfect franchise concept.
- Andreas Durst (AT&T, Zurich): Microsoft, has the market on its side. IBM, the market still buys the story and the charisma. Digital, for making probably the biggest turnaround in economic history, excellent products and people but poor management.

Every one of these companies is an exciting place to work, a true learning experience, with pilots and copilots in the cockpit who know where they are going, on an approved flight plan. Matching your own desires and needs to organizations like these—and there are many, many others, large and small—is the gold key to success for those who see the corporation as their way to their own career freedom.

KEY POINTS

Note: Chapter 8 (at the back of the book) has a complete set of checklists to help you think through your future career plans. This summary is designed to help you begin to think about the issues raised in this chapter.

1. There are three words that count in the new organizational work world: LEAN, MEAN, and FLAT. Make sure you follow them.

2. Training and communicating are the key to getting people in delayered organizations to working effectively: make sure that's what you and your corporation are investing in.

3. Don't forget, even in the smallest organization you will have to manage people to succeed. Technology helps but it doesn't take away responsibilities: invest in your interpersonal skills—those are the ones that will count double points in the future.

4. Steer clear of individuals and groups with negative ideas: make sure the people you work with win and win again.

5. Business needs a flexible task force and team and project leaders: learn how to be the best at that. Volunteer for programs and projects on the cutting edge of your organization's product line.

6. Remember to assess the top management in your corporation from time to time. Do they really know where they are going? Have they a flight plan for the future? Do your review every month. Make it a habit on the last Friday of the month, on the way home—it's a good idea.

7. If you are a woman trying to break into business, look honestly at where you work and ask, "Is this a male society?" If it is, sharpen your search criteria and start searching.

What You Should Do Now . . .

1. Take some time and ask yourself "What positive actions can I take, starting tomorrow? How can I add value to my organization AND get noticed for it?" Set yourself a series of priorities, expected results, and deadlines.

Priority One:
What it will achieve

_____

_____

_____

How to do it

_____

_____

_____

By when

_____

_____

Priority Two:

What it will achieve

_____

_____

_____

How to do it

_____

_____

_____

By when

_____

_____

Priority Three:

What it will achieve

_____

_____

_____

How to do it

_____

_____

_____

By when

_____

_____

2. Get to work on those interpersonal skills. Think about the ones you have AND (be honest) the ones you do not have. Make a plan to fill in the gaps. Check these out with a close friend or trusted work colleague.

Working with people I am BEST at:

_____
_____
_____
_____
_____

Working with people I am WORST at:

_____
_____
_____
_____
_____

Actions I can take to IMPROVE:

_____
_____
_____
_____
_____

Don't Wait for Someone Else to Help You

Any man who selects a goal in life that can be fully achieved has already defined his own limitations.

—CAVETT ROBERT

The creative person wants to be a know-it-all. He wants to know about all kinds of things: ancient history, nineteenth-century mathematics, current manufacturing techniques, flower arranging, and hog futures because he never knows when these might come together to form a new idea. It may happen in six minutes, six months, or six years down the road, but he has faith that it will happen.

—CARL ALLEY

Whatever your current situation, whether you are well placed within your organization, just starting out, or in some sort of mid-career crisis, there is one, single thing that all of us today must do to ensure a next chapter in our lives: learn to learn and like it too!

There has been a great deal of talk about learning: about what it is, what it is not, why we need to do it, and why those of us who work for organizations need to think that those same organizations are helping us to get new wisdom constantly. Most of us, hopefully, learn something new—however insignificant it may be—every day. It may have little or nothing to do with our work, but we usually learn something, we take on board information, and, using the critical faculties we have developed, we process it, catalog it, and, if important, act on it.

What is now being said is that we should apply what we do naturally to our work, or more importantly to our careers. You see, learning new ideas and new processes makes us better at what we do, creates a more valid and useful contribution, and—the biggest payoff—makes us employable.

Now there has been a great deal of discussion about companies entering the knowledge era and people being only as good as what they know. The commentators and business school professors say that the only thing that can differentiate one organization from another in today's highly competitive world is what the people it employs know AND continue to learn. To double buzzword it—in the knowledge era the learning organization is sitting pretty. At least that's another of the latest theories.

Yet once again, amidst this corporate storm we are going through, lots and lots of organizations are getting this terribly wrong: they are not really investing in their people at all, they are not even encouraging their people to learn. Just as we saw in the last chapter that companies seem to think you can empower people to do things by waving a magic wand and saying "Abracadabra you are now empowered," so they feel that they can confidently raise their heads high and fill the pages of the annual report with useless examples of being a learning organization. The learning organization does not exist. No CEO in the world can write in his or her annual report, "We are now a learning organization" for the very reason that a learning organization has tied up all its intellectual capital, all its knowledge, in the people it has—if it has already followed the rest of the instructions on the box. Look at it this way: if you are a newly empowered manager and your immediate boss or even the CEO has told you that he or she can no longer guarantee you a job, to whom do the knowledge and the ideas between your ears belong to? You, of course!

> *Learning new ideas and new processes ensures one thing—we stay employable.*

No organization can say "We can't offer you a contract for life; we cannot even offer you a guarantee for work until next year, but by the way we own your head." So the knowledge organization, the so-called learning organization, is actually one thousand, five thousand, or fifty thousand separate little entities, who can pack up and take their knowledge across the street, down the road, or around the corner to the competition. Because if you are an organization that wants to be flexible with the people you work with, you cannot hold their ideas to ransom when they are used up in your workplace. So the knowledge in the knowledge organization is never the same on any day, in any week, of any year. It is fluid and will stay that way as people come and go and as current employees add to their knowledge.

Imagine if you will that Bill Gates, founder of Microsoft, wakes up one morning with a great idea and decides to pack it all in and go join IBM. The intellectual capital of Microsoft drops like a lead brick—not to mention the stock price—as a lot of knowledge heads out the door.

So the first thing we must get straight in our minds is that our mind belongs to us. Maybe it didn't a decade ago when we sold out for promises of safety and a future, but in today's company it is very much your mind that you take to work every day and you take home again at night. At seven or eight o'clock in the evening, your company has zero knowledge because it has all gone home to dinner. All companies are inanimate objects. They don't live, they don't breathe—but you do. When you move, all your ideas, all your training, and all your learning move with you.

Therefore any learning and the new bells and whistles you add to your talent and your resume are yours—and yours alone.

 When you move, all your ideas, all your training, and all your learning move with you.

There are some corporations who deserve their reputation for keeping their people up to speed in the hope that this will give them a competitive advantage in the short, medium, and long term: General Electric and Motorola would both qualify for this accolade. The effort to keep up to date, and even far ahead, is being driven through individuals. If these individuals are not employable in the corporation in the future because of a variety of circumstances (getting out of a business, industry overcapacity, etc.), they can take those skills they have learned and auction themselves off to the highest bidder.

So the new thinking from the individual's point of view (from your point of view) has to be:

- What do I need to learn?
- Will my company help me?
- Where can I find one that will?

That approach will ensure that you stay competitive and have a longer and more fruitful career than most. And make no mistake about it, if the currency of capitalism has moved from money to minds, remember that minds—unlike money—are owned by the individuals involved. Just as a shareholder invests in a company with money, you invest your currency—your knowledge. But just as that shareholder can sell out at any time, so can you. It is no longer a corporate prerogative. A little too cynical? Not really. Look around you and see that within these inanimate, lifeless corporate entities even the people who are talking of the knowledge era and the learning organization are just that: people, ever ready to jump ship themselves and take their knowledge with them. Top managers move too, you know!

Within this new context of the way the working world operates— when you work *with* not *for* the corporation—your knowledge is the lifeblood of any corporation, group, network, or partnership you may enter into. So learning to learn and keeping that intellectual gas tank topped off gives you the range for cruising a lot of miles at top speed.

What Should You Be Learning?

But what exactly should you be learning to stay in tip-top shape and be one of those individuals that others want as an investor in their action? We could start with almost anything, but there are two important aspects: adding to your professional knowledge and becoming a more what used to be called well-rounded person. To use today's language, getting more of the vertical (professional and specialty) knowledge as well as the horizontal (the broader, organizationally focused, team leader–focused) knowledge is the ultimate goal. And forward-thinking organizations eager to stay ahead are certainly willing to help out in the process of knowledge acquisition.

However, before we examine that aspect of the learning process there are one or two basics that also need to be addressed. Catie Thorburn, an international director of the Club of Brussels, a strategy think-tank group, says that, in her experience, "there is one key piece of knowledge that most people fail to acquire—they just cannot string words together either sensibly or logically. Many of us," she points out, "are not really taught that, so throughout our lives we fail miserably to communicate—especially on paper—what our ideas are, what we really want to do." She's right. Look at anyone's resume and you'll find not just spelling errors but also an inability to make the best of what they've done. Company memoranda are also outstanding examples of muddled thinking and inarticulate arguments.

> *Learn how to communicate easily,*
> *fluently, and well.*

Want to get ahead? Learn how to communicate easily, fluently, and well.

Thorburn is equally scathing about what she sees as a total inability of schools and colleges to teach anything that has the remotest impact on our lives today. "Why," she admonishes, "are there no practical courses? We live off this stupid idea that thou shall get a college degree. What practical good does that do? Five languages and a specialization won't help you anymore either."

Her suggestion: "Let's have practical stuff in all the schools from age twelve onward. Let's teach the practical steps of survival: how to run a budget, how to appraise who you are and work on your weaknesses and strengths. Now that's something all of us could have used, instead of hoping we'd get lucky and be able to cope."

The view that we must change the basics if we are to change the new entrants into the job markets is supported by Neil Irons, managing partner of Hewitt/CBC in Brussels. He says that we must "change the focus of the education system. Beyond learning specific skills, children need to be taught learning skills, that is, skills like curiosity, adaptability, creativity, thinking outside of the box we are all squashed into. Above all," he says, "schools should be the prime place for making us grow in awareness of our own personalities; knowing and cultivating our own natures, styles, rhythms, tastes, and values. That is the strongest survival kit we can hand out to the new generation."

"Learning has to go way beyond what we've been taught," insists writer and presenter Tony Buzan. "Too much of what we are told is like giving advice to lemmings before they head for the cliff!" Buzan notes that much of what business has done has been wrongful as well. They gave people retirement training or told them to adjust their current skill; this isn't terribly useful in a shrinking market."

Indeed it is not. What you need is training and development to take hold of yourself, to check out the skill arsenal you possess and think how you can redirect it as required. As outplacement consultant Margaret Newborg in New York points out, "When you have a major loss of jobs like in the merger between Chase and Chemical banks, those jobs are gone forever. They are irreplaceable. But even though they have lost those jobs, there are pieces of their jobs, pieces of their knowledge, their learning, that they can put together to make them highly employable again in another business."

Buzan notes, "If you have been an accountant you don't go back to that, you go and learn—or hopefully you already know—new skills that your training in accounting will help you learn and you pack your bags and head for where demand is going up, not down."

Smart business leaders are realizing that you have to invest in people, even if they won't always be with you—that is the new currency as well as the new contract that the smart and the best will expect and demand. We must all demand it, because without it—without taking on board new skills and new ideas—we will find ourselves in free-fall if or when our organizational bubble bursts.

Organizational consultant Alf Chattell states, "Growth through learning is fast becoming the only insurance policy the individual has and a primary means by which individuals can exercise control over their own destiny. The once safe havens of the lifetime skills, organizational careers, and positions in the professions offer increasingly little shelter to decreasing numbers of people. Organizations that ask people to trade control over their destiny for a career with the organization will come under increasing scrutiny to see if they really are in a position to offer long-term careers at all. Few organizations can predict with any accuracy what they will look like in five years, never mind their requirements thirty or forty years ahead. Few of the organizations that we see around us now will be around in thirty or forty years anyway." Chattell continues, "Tomorrow, the contract between the organization and its people must become one of mutual growth, not the increasingly unreal one of the traditional career. As such, tomorrow's organizations must not ask or coerce people to give up control of their own destinies. If it does its people will feel threatened and go elsewhere." Coming back to his initial point that growth of the individual is the key, Chattell concludes, "Perhaps the ultimate reward for growth is a future-ensuring capacity for continuous self-renewal."

Certainly there is investment, with no strings attached, going on. Tony Buzan likes to recount the comments of one of his favorite CEOs, Richard Hunt of Burmah Petroleum, who tells his executives, "I am going to give you whatever training you need as long as it is to do with thinking. I won't always be here, and the passing of the baton when I go should be totally seamless: also if you have to change your career pattern that will be totally seamless." Others are using ongoing, nonstop training as a carrot to sign up new hires. A West Coast United States corporation is recruiting new people by saying, "This product line may exist for six or seven years, but no longer. However, we are offering you training facilities on a broad range of business skills from day one. When this product is finished, we cannot guarantee you a job, but with your newly acquired skills we will try our best. If we cannot employ you we will increase your separation payment by virtue of the fact that you accepted training and were willing to improve yourself from the beginning." This is the sort of offer (you could term it the new deal) that we should all be expecting to get from go-ahead, enlightened companies, which WILL be the places to work.

There is little doubt that such an investment in people produces a sense of value for the individual both inside and outside the organization. While some companies may lose out on "the best train for the rest" syndrome, most companies get back as much as they give. As DHL's Rob Kuijpers says, "In our eastern European operations we are training very young managers all the time. Many of them leave and end up heading Hungarian, Czech, and Polish companies. They also become our most loyal customers."

It seems inevitable, therefore, that organizations that expect to succeed must give training to their people and encourage them to take it. Training may take the form of evening classes, time off during the work week, self-study—even a sabbatical. What is clear is that those companies that do this will attract the best people. And those people, secure in the knowledge they are at the front of the pack, will work better, knowing that this is at one and the same time keeping them more attractive to the current company and an attractive catch when, or if, they leave.

A Word about the Work Ethic

If we are all being urged to learn, to change our human currency from sweat to smarts, this presumes that all of us—or at least the majority of us—have the necessary mind-set to devote our time to getting better. However, at the same time we hear and read a lot about the work ethic not being around anymore—that proud thing our parents and grandparents had that made them get up in the morning. We see TV programs and read magazine articles about people who don't want to work or want to work fewer hours. Many blame this on poor examples set by parents, who fail to instill in their offspring any sense of duty. Others add that schools and turning away from organized religion must bear some of the responsibility.

> *We have to change our human currency*
> *from sweat to smarts.*

In our Western society, most experts seem to think that we have a great number of problems to solve and that there are no easy answers. It might be fine between the pages of a management book to talk about self-motivation and self-actualization and only working for organizations that are going to invest in your future as you invest in theirs, but if you haven't got a job and have little prospect of getting one the future is bleak indeed. What appears to be happening is that parents, themselves the victims of long-term unemployment or poor casual work patterns, are unable to give any vision of hope or drive to their children. Rundown inner cities and towns with closed-down smokestack industry, where the *raison d'être* for being there in the first place has long gone, are mute witnesses to this. Many see this as a government problem, but it is unlikely to be solved quickly or easily. In countries like Spain, where unemployment runs over 25 percent nationwide and hits 40 percent in some depressed pockets, there is simply no work nor the prospect of any for some. Southern Belgium, northern France, northeast England—once boom areas in the industrial revolution and the age of coal and iron—have been going downhill since the last war, with zero prospects for more than token inward investment. It is in these areas of most need that the least is being done.

As Linda Holbeche of Roffey Park Management Institute sadly relates, "I guess that many young people will be aware of the current realities because of what they see happening to their parents. Currently the young people who seem to have the strongest work ethic are the ones who are most focused on getting a first job and then being skilled at leveraging that to maximize their opportunities. Often these are people from professional, middle-class backgrounds, but that is not always the case." She goes on, "Success these days seems to require people to be more competitive than their counterparts of thirty years ago, and for many young people a ruthless desire to succeed goes counter to their ideals." Holbeche offers one idea: "Maybe employers need to find ways to encourage young people to see the world a bit before they appoint first-time job seekers. In this way everyone would win, as young employees would bring a more mature approach to their work."

But will cost-conscious companies ever take up a challenge like that? Even the most socially responsible would probably balk at anything more than a short-term commitment, and that would do little to alleviate a long-term issue.

Finally, Holbeche predicts, "Certainly parents and schools can do a lot to encourage children to become more self-reliant and responsible as well as teaching them key transferable skills—teamworking, interpersonal relations, and flexibility. Also, the opportunity to have work experience as teenagers no doubt helps." While others echo Linda Holbeche's worries and feeling of powerlessness to do all that much, there is another, more radical view on this from Asia. Tokyo-based consultant and author T.W. Kang notes that "this is one area where Asia is strong and I think that one reason for this aggressive work ethic, common to many of the economically dynamic Asian nations, is Confucianism. Confucianism is to religion as Latin is to language. It is not practiced anymore, and therefore it is more of a philosophy than a religion. I honestly think that Westerners would do well to try and understand Confucianist principles much more than in the past. While they would probably not desire to and should not blindly adopt it, I believe that a more than cursory look at this different way of doing things may provide a hint for the reinvention of the currently deteriorating work ethic in many parts of the West."

What Do Tomorrow's Executives Think?

Linda Holbeche's uncomfortable point that many of our future managers will come from parents who have a strong work ethic, and many of them from middle-class backgrounds, does tend to strike the right note; however, many of us would wish it otherwise. Her other point, that success at any price, the trait that drove so many ambitions until the last recession, is not as strong, certainly appears to be true. Not that the work ethic is dead; it is just a different viewpoint from those at the beginning of their career rather than those already on their way. The ME generation can be declared officially dead.

Those in college or university today and those just graduated have been brought up since they first started to be conscious of the economic and social world around them, ten or so years ago, with an acute awareness that it isn't boom time for jobs—far from it. Consequently many have lowered their ambitions and expectations before they even embark on a career.

To see if this were true, I polled two groups of young people. The first were recent graduates, all with degrees, who responded to an advertisement in a Belgian newspaper for trainee managers at Carlson Wagonlit, Belgium's leading business travel group. The firm had placed the ad to fill four openings; they received over 450 replies—an indication of the difficulty in finding a job in Belgium in 1996. Every candidate had a graduate degree and spoke fluent Dutch, French, and English; most knew German as well.

What to do with 450 potential candidates? Carlson Wagonlit had an idea. Why not rent an auditorium and invite them all to come for an interview. Eventually, a more sane approach prevailed and they had a first cut, ending up with just over one hundred.

I created a questionnaire that each job applicant had to complete in English as part of the interview process. Here are some of the responses:

- Virtually all of them saw their future with a large multinational or a large national corporation. Reasons ranged from "I think they guarantee better opportunities and training for the future" to "greater chances to grow and be promoted."
- Very few had any desire to become an entrepreneur or work for themselves, although a few said they might consider it after they had some experience in a company that they could put to use. Reasons included "I want a family life," "I'm not adventurous and I need security," and "not prepared to take a financial risk."
- The majority said that they would be quite happy to stay with the same company for their entire career, assuming there were some prospects for advancement; practically 20 percent actually cited "loyalty to the company" as a factor.
- Over 90 percent stressed that there was little chance of getting any employer to hire you if you didn't have some work experience. Sitting on your duff in the summer was not a good idea at all.

- Job content and satisfaction were cited in all cases as more important than salary, even in the long term.
- The idea of long work hours and a long commute morning and evening would put quite a few off taking a job, but most said they could put up with it if they were getting relevant experience they could use in the future.
- The wild work ethic of anything to make money is gone.

Despite the shortage of entry-level jobs for graduates in Europe these days, it seems that the wild work ethic of anything to make money is gone. Also it seemed, in this group at least, that few had heard the stories that midsized companies were providing most of the job growth (a fact as true in Belgium as anywhere else) and seemed naively unaware or unconcerned about the swinging job losses in large industries. True, their linguistic ability gives them more opportunities than others, but their lack of realization that Belgium has had a huge net loss of jobs and is hosting a shrinking number of multinational corporations was a little disturbing. A senior advertising agency executive later explained a possible reason for this: "Young people don't read newspapers, they listen to the radio (where most advertising francs end up these days), which has sound-bite news and no analysis." He may well be right; it's certainly true that you don't get much insight into your nation's economic situation from a rhythm-and-blues station or zapping into MTV.

The second group interviewed were all students at Amsterdam's prestigious Erasmus University. Of various nationalities, they were all in the international affairs program; their responses echoed and amplified those of the Belgian group.

- Yes, they all felt that work experience during their studies was vital. "It's almost as important as the qualification itself," said one.
- Yes, the job content was vital. "Money means nothing to me," said one respondent. Others echoed that sentiment or felt they would never be in what one called "lucrative employment."
- Seeing what they produced was ten times more important than simply seeing figures on a paper or a VDU. "To produce something of worth and value that can be reflected upon. This would encourage me to produce something else of a higher standard."
- Long hours and a difficult commute would depend on the job. "I wouldn't travel twenty miles to pack meat, but I'd work as long as it would take to complete something I believe in." Another re-

ports, "I wouldn't mind as long as I got compliments on having done the job well and people are glad they can work with me."
- In this group, the split was between a big multinational (because it afforded great training and a better career track) and small companies (because they are friendlier) and working for themselves.
- Some saw themselves eventually running their own business. "I could do things how and when I want," suggested one student, but others were discouraged by the risk factor.

This group seemed more aware of the ebbs and flows of business and the consequent opportunities, but the focus on multinationals again shows that there has been little penetration of the news that they have been shedding people like a dog sheds hair.

It would appear from talking with and researching these two groups that the work ethic is still there, but it is different, changed considerably from ethics even a decade older. There were no blatantly ambitious men or women in either interview. What this will mean for the future is anyone's guess, but once they get jobs and begin to discover something more about market forces things might change. One thing is clear though. Employers who think they can get away with hiring intelligent, young future managers at any price couldn't be more wrong. These future managers are looking for an investment to be made in them as much as any other employee, perhaps even more so.

Here Comes the Renaissance

However, the attitude about jobs held by students—a refusal to take a job at any price no matter what—may well be the right one for the next age we are entering. Someone who thinks that is Tony Buzan, who promotes the idea that "nations, governments, and individuals get frantic when unemployment rises and one reason they do that is because the word 'unemployment' is inextricably linked to the word 'gainfully.' " And that gainful employment, says Buzan, "means standard manufacturing, standard service, nine to five, five days a week for a standard wage." But in this new world, this new age we are entering, that is not the right way to see things, although how you can begin to try and persuade governments to take another view is hard to imagine. But, says

Buzan, they must, because he strongly believes in a new age that will support the arrival of a true renaissance manager. Buzan explains it this way: "Virtually all utopian visions have been totally the opposite of the way we live today: no one worked, everyone played. Like the Greek and Italian renaissance they are devoted to the mind, to physical things, to art and sport." Buzan reckons that in our developed societies at least we are entering a new renaissance ("just look at all the magazines, they are all about leisure"). "We are misreading the signs," he claims, "and seeing as bad these changes to our life, when actually we have reached the point, in many parts of Western culture, where we can support these types of activity, because an increasingly large number of people can live without working." Buzan is not talking of the hard-core unemployed; he is talking about people who are well enough off not to worry if they work or not or only work a little to maintain mental interest.

Buzan's idea may seem utopian, but then again a new renaissance would take time to be seen. A new renaissance wouldn't mean all of us walking around in frock coats and wigs speaking Latin and Greek. It would be Bob, Bill, and Charlie at fifty-five years old saying, "Why go back to work? We've got enough saved to live on if I take my pension early." In fact, in the United States at least (a country with over a million millionaires), outplacement firms report just that: newly downsized employees over fifty often don't want to go back to full-time employment because they just don't need it. The mobile workforce that built America seems to have passed into history—a relic of an earlier economic shakeout when people were less cushioned than today.

In Europe, the coming inheritance boom—on which little hard research has focused—will create the same situation. Literally millions of forty- and fifty-year-olds, right this minute, are inheriting undreamed of sums from their parents. This is creating a new upper-middle class of wealthy who don't need work—or at least don't need full-time work—to support their life-style. For the first time in more than two centuries Germans are inheriting from their parents. With property values high they can sell homes and pocket the money, freeing them from major financial worries forever. Elsewhere across Europe and in North America, millions of baby-boomers are entering their late forties and early fifties with an inheritance from their parents, who were part of the postwar boom, when the middle class expanded and home ownership mushroomed. For many of these people, that money provides a new freedom to do a lot of the things they wanted to accomplish; nine-to-five (and often much longer) five days a week, on and off planes, and a two-hour commute aren't part of that new third-age agenda.

If you just look at the new settlers on the Mediterranean coastline (Scandinavian, British, German, Swiss, and the like) from the Portuguese Algarve to Greece, you will find a commonality of age that begins in the early fifties. Fit, mobile, and moneyed, they are a new class that hasn't been seen before, because there are so many of them. With rapid advances in telecommunications, they can also work—if they choose to—in locations unheard of even twenty years ago doing jobs unheard of five years ago.

> *Today you can work in a location impossible twenty years ago at a job unheard of five years ago.*

While this may well create an ever bigger gap in our society between the haves and the have-nots, it will also take a lot of people out of the workforce or create a totally fresh series of job opportunities. And with shrinking or even negative birthrates in most of Western society, these people may be a godsend, leaving jobs that can be eagerly grabbed by the new graduates entering our working world.

But while Buzan and others may be right that these changes will bring about a revolution, governments are still finding it almost impossible to break the "contracts" they promised us. Sadly, many are living in a fool's paradise because, already bankrupt, they have no chance of ever meeting their obligations to individuals in their crippled social systems. The best advice that I have heard on this subject is "Whatever you do, don't ever plan on receiving an old-age pension from any government anywhere, and certainly don't think you'll ever get back what you put in."

Can Government Do Anything at All?

In Europe in particular, government has an impossible task to deal with. Over the whole of the European Union (EU) the unemployment average is just under 11 percent: just over eighteen million people. The EU is trying to get people back to work, but such is the complication of legislation—and the mix from member state to member state—that many of its efforts are frustrated. Reports the Economic Policy Committee of the EU in a 1995 paper titled "Member States' Progress with Unemployment Policies," "Structural labor market measures, by their nature, take some time for their effects to become apparent and the identification of the more recent successful policies is not a straightforward task. Further, labor market problems vary between member states and action across a number of fronts in any one country does not necessarily suggest that all difficulties have been removed."

The report goes on, "Even so, all member states are actively pursuing policies to improve the functioning of their labor markets and several member states are able to identify policies judged to be successful in areas such as improving wage flexibility, improving vocational and other training, job placement schemes, flexibility in working time and reductions in indirect labor costs, particularly for those countries where unemployment among the lower paid is a problem."

The Economic Policy Committee then adds, "However, we also note that much more action is needed across a wide number of areas, including employment protection legislation, improving geographical and sectoral mobility, and tightening and enforcing social benefit entitlement rules."

In other words—as far as governments really helping to reduce those numbers and helping to drive the renaissance of a new working world—they are in one hell of a mess and frankly are not getting anywhere.

Even they admit that. A few paragraphs later, the report concludes, "Whilst employment is rising and unemployment in the Union is beginning to decline somewhat, it must be expected however, that much of the initial improvement is the normal, cyclical response of employment to the growth in economic activity. Hence, this is only a beginning—perhaps a fragile one—and there is a long way to go."

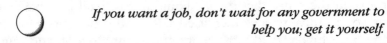

> *If you want a job, don't wait for any government to help you; get it yourself.*

What this statement really says, when viewed with a cynical eye, is "Wow, we thought we had done a lot, but actually we are back where we started."

The advice, therefore, is if you want a job, don't stand around and wait for the government—European, American, state, city, or whatever—to help you. You might get lucky; chances are you won't.

However, the big issue, and one that does need to be understood, is the trade-off between the supply side of the labor market and the demand side. Both supply side and demand side are plagued with problems, largely due to the following factors:

- People who work hard and earn lots of money also pay lots of tax—in most of Europe at least.
- People who don't work at all get too much assistance and lose the incentive to work, and certainly the incentive to relocate in order to get a job.
- Tax structures decrease the willingness of people to work more hours or drive them into the black economy.
- Employers won't take on new hires because it costs too much in nonwage costs (social security payments) and termination costs in a business downturn (this applies specifically to Europe).

Let's see what the EU's Economic Policy Committee thinks about these issues.

According to another paper, "Social Benefits, Taxation and the Labor Market, in 1995," "concerning the supply side of the labor market, the following efficiency problems arise:

- For those out of work, social benefits may result in high net replacement ratios that, when combined with long durations on benefit, may weaken the incentive to engage in active job search, thus producing longer spells in receipt of benefit. This increases the risk of creating a hard core of long-term unemployed.
- For those who take up a low-paid job, supplemented with in-work benefits, additional gross earnings can lead to high implicit marginal tax rates via the onset of income taxes, employee social security charges, and benefit withdrawal. This creates poverty traps, in the sense that those taking up low-paid jobs have little or no incentive to seek increased skills and productivity in order to obtain higher paid jobs. Economic, technological, and regulatory barriers often lock such individuals into low-productivity jobs with limited alternative opportunities. Poverty traps reduce incentives and labor mobility and have adverse effects on structural employment.

- The structure of personal income taxation may affect the individual's willingness to increase the number of hours worked or perhaps to take up a job in the official economy; this is likely to affect, in particular, part-time employees. More generally, high effective marginal rates of taxation affect not only the size of registered labor supply but also the effectiveness of this labor supply as they can contribute to high rates of structural unemployment."

If the supply side makes depressing reading, let's take a look at what the committee reports of the employer's view of the situation and that impact on our society.

"Turning to the demand side, problems relate to:

- An employer's willingness to hire people responds to the evolution of total labor costs. Indirect, or nonwage costs, may constrain the employer's willingness to create jobs, to the extent that such costs are (a) not perceived as being part of labor's total remuneration and (b) because they are intrinsically less variable and responsive to the economic cycle, at least in the short run.
- Both analysis and empirical evidence suggest that lower-skilled labor is particularly affected by a relatively higher rigidity in total labor costs, given that many nonwage cost components are not proportional to wages.
- In order to avoid creating a class of working poor through widening the wage scale, the commission's White Paper has recommended that lower indirect labor costs be realized through targeted reductions in employer's social security contributions as a policy priority.
- In addition, some analysis suggests that benefits that are too generous may generate a wage floor that compresses the wage distribution and locks out the lower skilled from employment. Further an excessive burden of taxation on labor may affect negatively the overall level of employment, induce too much capital deepening, and also harm price competitiveness in international markets. Also, there are stronger incentives to engage in fraud and to increase the size of the black economy."

Having faced this doom and gloom, the EU then compares the mess it is in with that of the United States.

"Comparisons are often drawn," they say, "with the United States, in which its smaller welfare state may help in explaining its superior job creation record. However, this feature of the U.S. economy has been accompanied by important equity problems, due to downward pressure on real earnings for the lower skill groups, a widening earnings distribution [the wage gap], and the creation of a class of people who are in work but nevertheless have very low incomes. Indeed, recent reforms in the United States have extended the social protection system somewhat in order to tackle the emergence of these social imbalances."

On the evidence of the EU's efforts and that of its individual states, it would seem inevitable that there will be a growth of the divide between the poor and the rich and that even the brightest people in government are still lost as to what real action to take.

As the EU concludes, "The broad systems in the Community [the EU] suggest the question of policy tradeoffs between an employment trap, which reduces incentives to work, and a poverty trap, reducing incentives to seek higher skills and better-paid jobs. Some acceptable balance between the two has to be found. At this stage the Committee can offer no clear answer to the question as to which strategy offers the best solution to higher employment and prosperity."

To be cruel, all this rhetoric means that little is going to get done that will positively affect people on the lower end of the scale or even those that don't have the ability to self-help or access to private enterprise assistance (career counseling, outplacement, and so on). Certainly in interviews most business observers have little time for government, believing that its policies are often seen as ill-informed interference or out of touch with the smoking fuse of social unrest that's ready to explode if they don't come up with some answers and some action soon.

What this information confirms is that learning to learn and portability of skills are going to be the reality for the well-educated minority, not the struggling low-paid, unemployed, and disenfranchised.

Here are the thoughts of Don Bates of Sumner Rider: "Smart governments will get people together to talk about their problems and solutions or risk building the stockpile of social dynamite in their midst. Since it won't just be the lower classes out of work and stressed by the challenges of today's disintegrating world in the future, it will be a lot more difficult for governments to maintain control of their domains. The have-nots won't be as docile or as easy to contain as in the past because their legions will be composed of people from all walks of life."

An equally worried view is put forth by Brussels-based publisher David Starr: "Governments are already doing what they can; I don't believe that anything further is possible, given inherent limitations of self-interest and intellect." Starr adds, "The fact that many Western countries will soon have unemployment over 20 percent [some already have] will be more than an issue: it will bring about the most sweeping changes in society and government since World War II and hold enormous promise of great harm. No one will escape."

American Tom McGuire, founder of Clarus, an international marketing consultancy in Brussels, who created a major stir in 1995 with an article in the *Wall Street Journal-Europe* berating the Belgian government for its punitive stance on social security that was, he opined, a major disincentive to getting people back to work, has three ideas for getting things to move:

- Governments should liberalize local labor legislation. This means more flexibility to hire and fire, greater chances for part-time and temporary work, and reduced financial penalties for employers who lay off workers. Unemployment in the EU is around 11 percent, about twice the level of the United States. Why? In a word, U.S. labor law is more flexible and less structured toward safeguarding cradle-to-grave employment, including commensurate social benefits. Transactions between companies and the workforce need to be more free, friendly, and fair in order to meet the changes and challenges of the 1990s. Governments should make it easier to incentivize good workers and less complicated and costly to get rid of bad ones.
- Governments should enact less oppressive personal and corporate tax regimes. Less government spending and more private resourcefulness would suit the emerging economy of the Western industrialized world, which is increasingly marked by mobility, internationally defined products and services, and information-intensive business activities.
- Governments should initiate new ideas in concert with industry with regard to setting up new businesses and growing existing ones. This means tax incentives, reduced barriers to hiring and firing, and increased investment by local authorities to train and develop youth. Innovation means that governments reduce risk for entrepreneurs and improve rewards for investing in plant, people, and profitable performance.

McGuire's arguments need a wider audience than this book and a more ongoing campaign to articulate them fully and press for

Key Points

Note: Chapter 8 (at the back of the book) has a complete set of checklists to help you through your future career plans. This summary is designed to help you begin to think about the issues raised in this chapter.

1. Learn to learn and learn to like it. It's going to make you EMPLOYABLE: change your personal currency from SWEAT to SMARTS.

2. Learning organizations are a public relations myth. Organizations don't learn, people do, and they quit, get fired, and go home each night: remember, you own your own knowledge—USE IT!

3. Learn how to communicate verbally AND how to write. These are two basic skills that most of us still don't excel in.

4. Even first-time job seekers won't take just any position. Today job content is valued above pay and prospects.

5. Don't expect your government to help you in your career development or job search—chances are it won't.

6. For some, technology has created freedom of work location, but beware, it isn't for everyone.

What You Should Do Now . . .

1. Do an honest assessment of yourself (as in previous chapters) of what you still need to know to become an attractive job candidate or a candidate for a new position or promotion.

What are the areas of my knowledge NOW?

_____

_____

_____

_____

_____

What are the areas where I need to add/increase my knowledge?

_____

_____

_____

_____

_____

What actions can I take (courses, self-study, work experience etc.) that will help me achieve this?

_____

_____

_____

_____

_____

2. Ask friends or trusted work colleagues to give you an honest assessment of your oral and written communication skills. If you need to improve these (and most of us do), enroll in an effective writing or effective presentation skills program.

Getting Out

Don't be irreplaceable. If you can't be replaced, you can't be promoted.
—ANONYMOUS

A wise man knows everything; a shrewd one, everybody.
—ANONYMOUS

In the French language *travail* means work. Oddly, in English the travails of our life are translated into adversity, trouble, and worries, which tend these days to be associated with having no work. But whether we lose our job or *nous avons perdu notre travail* the effects are similar: there is a traumatic time ahead, no matter what hard exterior we present to the world.

Everyone is at risk these days, even those of us who feel we may well be in secure positions. Changing work patterns, cutthroat competition from a new entrant in the market, mergers and acquisitions, even a new boss with different ideas—all these can happen at the snap of the fingers. These days you don't have a lot of time to see changes coming at you. In this just-in-time world you are trussed up and tied onto the track at 6:14, one minute before the 6:15 train comes out of the tunnel and runs you over.

All right, there are ways to see what might happen, to get a glimmer of what is going on, but how many of us, fearful of taking the plunge into those shark-infested waters described by Adrian Furnham in chapter 1, are honest enough with ourselves to admit the company we work for is in trouble or, worse still, are too scared to find out what the reality really is?

It really isn't that difficult to see, and, as I keep stressing, keeping a regular watching brief on how the organization you are in now performs is not a bad idea. At least it gets you out and over the cliff before the rest, so you can choose where you swim before the feeding frenzy starts.

For example, look at the company you work for or the one you plan to work for and think about these pointers. In fact, take a pencil and put a Yes or No beside each one.

- Do you know the share price today, and do you know if the trend is up or down?
- Have you read about the organization in the news recently? Are they hiring or firing? Do they have any new products or services? Are they redefining their strategy by closing offices and plants? If they are, what about where you live?
- Have you a friend in headquarters who can give you the real news of what's going on?
- Are senior managers beginning to leave? Has there been any major top management shake-ups in recent months?
- If you ask your manager or supervisor what's going on, does he or she answer "How should I know?"
- Are personal training and development being cut to bare essentials?
- Being frank, is there a positive or negative feel to the place?

After an honest assessment, if you are coming up with too many negatives to too many of these questions, it really is time to go. It is time for you to recognize that in the transitions to new working methods that we are all being asked to make, your organization isn't going to be in the first division for very much longer.

 It's time to go when you see senior managers leaving and shakeouts at the top.

On the other hand, if the organization looks pretty darn good, all things considered, you might want to do your best to stay. If that's the case, then, as we have already pointed out, if you're not in a growth area already, try to get into one. Unless you have severe personal limitations that preclude it, let it be known that you are quite prepared to move—nationally or internationally—if needed.

Business writer and consultant John Humble, author of the hugely influential book *Management by Objectives* written in the 1970s, suggests a few objectives to keep in mind for those who, having assessed their company's prospects, decide that their career should remain firmly right where it is now: "Those who recognize the dangers early on and try to stack the odds in their favor are going to be the winners. They are the ones that say, 'Well, if 20 percent of the managers in this place have to go anyway, one of them isn't going to be me!' "

According to Humble, there are five key elements to helping you get additional security, even if managers all around you are losing theirs.

- Be outstanding in the performance of your present job. Hard, measurable results, sustained over time, are a rock-solid foundation for security. Determine to be the best!
- Continuously enlarge your competence: if you are a commercial lawyer, make sure you study and become the source of best knowledge in your firm on marketing or some other new competence. Also keep ahead in your professional field, attend professional meetings, read journals, and attend training courses.
- Identify ways to improve your job and put these ideas forward in a thorough and objective way. In reality, only a minority of managers bother to do this. You will be noticed and appreciated. (If not, it's back to the early-jump-over-the-cliff option!)
- Hard work: deserve the reputation as a manager totally committed to the success of your job and your firm.
- Build good performing people in your team. Be generous in praising them and building their careers. Don't forget—you cannot succeed on your own.

Don Bates, executive vice president of public relations firm Sumner Rider in New York, agrees with Humble: "Become a damn expert in the business your employer runs. Become so damn knowledgeable and skilled that it will be that much more of an effort for the company to let you go."

Make Sure That the Network's Alive

Humble also advises that nothing stays good forever, so you not only have "to accept your own responsibility for managing your own career, but you must network like hell. Build up the widest group of people you can. They are invaluable for two things: learning and support in adversity."

But Humble's point about networks and doing things for yourself—back to the "We must all be self-reliant theme"—also raises another issue: your self-reliance. Your network should be a positive factor that your company should appreciate. Inward-looking employees, who have little contact with the outside environment, are an anathema to any company and much more so today. Employees who turn up at nine, leave at five, and take forty-five-minute lunches IN the staff restaurant are, by their very nature, going to abhor change and be about as flexible as a dry spaghetti noodle.

What corporations need today are people with an outward look, an inquiring, investigative, and open mind, who know people. If you know people, you either know how to do something or can get hold of someone who can. Having a strong network should be a plus factor that any smart employer would look for.

> *Keep good performers on your team; you cannot succeed on your own.*

All of us, no matter how well we keep ourselves prepared, are vulnerable. "Anyone who doesn't know this in their heart of hearts is an ostrich," says New York career counselor and outplacement consultant Bill Ayers.

But there were—probably still are—a lot of ostriches around. So many in fact that Ayers' firm was asked by client companies to devise an employee program to get the "we are all vulnerable" message across to what Ayers calls "their valued, long-time troops, with unfortunate delusions of entitlement."

Titled "Making the Most of Change in Your Career," the seminar raised the following issues:

- What have you learned in the past year that augments your career-related skills (technical, managerial, on-the-job learning)?
- What personal skills development program, if any, do you have in mind?
- What professional or trade organizations do you belong to and are you a current, active member?
- Has your Rolodex (or other contact file system) grown in the last year and, if so, by how much? If not, why not?
- Do you have a systematic approach to keeping in touch with your existing professional network? If so, what is it? If not, why not?
- As an employee, have you considered a lateral move within your company that would help you learn new skills and acquire new

knowledge? Have you worked with new people and solved new problems? What possibilities exist?

This process gets people into an "I'm-in-charge-of-myself" mode and can have long-term positive consequences. In some cases it helps employers identify people they had passed over or lost interest in. In another it makes employees face up to the new realities.

We are all vulnerable. We have all heard and read time and time again that we cannot be guaranteed a job for life. OK, maybe your

---

NEW JOBS FOR OLD

What type of jobs do people land after they go through the outplacement process? The answer is all sorts. And they are jobs, clearly defined and action focused.

Erik Hoffmoen of Oslo-based Institutt for Karriereutvikling says that new jobs they are placing candidates in "typically have a more direct content—more doing than managing, more direct customer contact, and greater accountability."

He goes on to give an example of this. "A young senior executive in a financial services operation had the position of operations manager with thirty people reporting to him. It would have been possible for the person to perform the job from his office as a staff person. He did not choose this role but took part in query and complaint resolution with direct customer contact. After his firm underwent a business process reengineering project, he became redundant. He has now landed a job as the managing director of a small, fast-growing, successful company selling slimming products. After some reconciliation that he had just left a high-status company in a business area that carried considerable prestige, he accepted the new position because it gave him full accountability and the opportunity to develop through his own resources: doing business, exercising leadership, being customer-oriented, not just managing a process."

Hoffmoen adds, "These are the streetwise objectives that many people are seeking and knowing they have to develop after having worked in staff roles or inside a detailed web of rules and guidelines. In this case our candidate, although he initially had preferred to see himself in a division of a larger company, felt his career objectives, as he wanted to define them, had been met."

Herbert Muhlenhoff of Mulenhoff & Partner in Dusseldorf reports, "We were taking care of a chemical engineer in his midfifties who had had a very successful and long career stretch with a multinational

company. Following the closure of their fiber business he began looking for a similar position with our assistance. Despite his personal,
positive attributes, he did not even get close to a job offer. The chemical business at that time was under great pressure. However, this was
at the time when former East German combines were beginning the
process of cleaning up their hazardous waste. He got in touch with
some West German consulting firms offering his expertise in chemical plants and was sent as a project manager to two of the major
chemical sites. He tremendously enjoys his rather unorthodox work,
the unfamiliar surroundings, and the opportunity to create something new."

Muhlenhoff cites another example of a senior executive in the advertising industry. "After his first dismissal, the job search was relatively easy, but his new employment did not last long. A sudden staff
reduction resulted in a last-in, first-out situation. The thought of going freelance was in the air but was viewed with hesitation. It took a
while, but then the first big assignment came in. Now there is no
question of him ever returning to an organization: business is steady,
customers are happy, and he highly values the freedom to make his
own decisions and mistakes."

Daniel Leroux of PCM in Paris explains how a sales manager for
an EDP service has set up and manages a network of EDP consultants
who all work on a freelance basis. "He takes charge of their contract
negotiation, administration, and payroll as well as their ongoing
technical education requirements. The consultants get to devote virtually 100 percent of their time to their work and do not have the
worry of low workloads. He charges a percentage of the total billings
of each individual."

From Madrid, Felipe Uria of Arco Creade recounts how a fifty-year-
old managing director in the cement business found himself out of
work due to the crisis in the country's building industry. "His first
move, typical of many successful professionals, was to contact several
head-hunting companies in Barcelona and Madrid, " says Uria. "He
was cordially received but politely told in no uncertain terms that in
the current economic situation his age and sector of experience
made him a difficult candidate to place."

Uria continues the story. "Together with his outplacement consultant he revised his strategy and began to work his personal network,
which was quite extensive thanks to his involvement in counseling
troubled couples through a local church group. Working the network
requires you to be clear about what you have to offer, but he was an
excellent manager, had highly developed interpersonal skills, and
knew the construction market inside and out. He was looking for a
position where he could put these strengths into play. His new job
lead when it came was from an unlikely source—the priest at his local

church! A private foundation that was sponsoring the restoration of religious monuments needed someone to oversee and manage the complex project. Our client was successful in landing the job not only because he was highly qualified technically but also because of his special abilities in dealing with people, as the job meant he would be in contact with high-ranking church and local government officials as well as the media."

Felipe Uria concludes, "The job brought a 30 percent pay reduction over his previous position. Yet his work with his outplacement consultant in taking the time to clarify his new values let him realize that salary was not the number one concern for evaluating a new job. A generous severance package from his ex-company and the fact that his children had completed their university studies had reduced his monetary requirements."

Frank Ebbinge of Slooter & Partners in The Hague describes another success story of a former line manager in a major Dutch research institute who faced starting a new career at fifty-seven years old. "He started his own consultancy firm, advising on the latest technical developments in his field. He was hugely successful because he had a colossal network that he had kept carefully up to date all his working life."

Ebbinge's colleague Lilian Margadant adds another. "A female employee of a transport company was asked to leave the organization at the age of fifty-one after a reorganization but mainly because of regular, unacceptable days off for illness. We advised her on suitable medical help and when she was better we counseled her. She changed dramatically from a very timid, sickly person when she entered the program to a confident, proactive woman, fully in change of her own life. Her health had improved drastically, so much so that her former company decided to take her back and offered her a better position."

Bill Ayers of the Ayers Group in New York gives another example of an exciting life-after-death case. "A senior executive, originally downsized from a major health insurer after a seven-year career there subsequently had a series of what turned out to be two-year assignments at other health care providers. The mandates of these subsequent jobs were to set up managed health care programs so that the companies could compete in the current marketplace. When the assignment was sufficiently on track so that the permanent staff could continue on a care and maintenance basis, the executive left her 'silver bullet' on the mantel and moved on to the next challenge."

In getting that new job, another thing to keep in mind is finding a mentor who can help the transition process, especially if your industry has little to offer and you need to change direction quickly to a growth business. Here's an example from Bill Ayers. "Some of our best candidates have acquired a mentor (either through us or on their own) who was willing to make introductions. This worked especially well with one of our candidates who wanted to switch from packaged goods marketing to health care marketing. Her counselor introduced her to a senior executive in the health care field who gave the candidate a quick primer on the industry, people, buzzwords, and research she had to do in order to be seen as a viable candidate. She subsequently landed a job as head of marketing for a hospital, which would have taken a lot longer and been a much more difficult process without the mentor's help."

What these examples show is that being made redundant isn't the end of the world, just a new beginning. Keeping networks operational is a key, as is facing up to the fact that you don't necessarily have to go back to the same level of responsibility, stress, or salary. What you do need is a full and thorough self-assessment of what your needs really are.

employer hasn't told you that, but we all know what's going on. Frankly, if we don't face up to it now—if we stick our heads in the proverbial sand—we practically deserve what we get.

If you are employed and intend to stay that way, the network that you build up inside and outside your place of work needs to have one special element. In order to plug into the neural center of your organization, you need a spy at corporate HQ. Now if it's a Fortune 500 company and you are in, say, Frankfurt, knowing what's happening at European HQ will help—until the Euro-HQ gets downsized out of existence, as the current trends seem to indicate. So it will be better if you can plug into the real powerhouse, where all the real decisions, bad and good, get made. E-mail (at least in companies that don't screen it) is highly effective and costs almost nothing. If you are working your own network right, you'll have your own computer at home; even if you're broke, you can get a good secondhand one for less than a stereo system.

Knowing what's coming down the pike has always been the most important thing for individuals as well as companies, and getting a head start on what might be happening gets you prepared in advance. Then this is where the network kicks in. It might not be that nice to face up to the fact that you are going to have to jump out of the blazing building, but knowing you'll have to means you can have your network—like a safety net—waiting down below to catch you. Bad as the news is, choosing your own window to jump out of and deciding how far to fall is a lot less gut-wrenching than the "I never knew a thing until it happened" syndrome.

Of course, short-circuiting the in-company information system can have far-reaching consequences. A late night call from a New York coworker to a colleague in Paris ensured that three layers of middle management knew just which departments were on the line hours before European top management had the details. In fact they found out because a Parisian headhunter called up his top management buddy to see if he needed some help to find a job (at least part of the senior executive's survival network was operating)!

Being in the First Lifeboat Off the Sinking Ship

Being informed about what's happening does one thing—it gets you a ticket for the first lifeboat. And that's an important invitation to have. Studies show that Lifeboat One has two attributes. The people in Lifeboat One get new jobs, because the news isn't out that the XYZ Corporation is imploding. They also—in virtually all cases—get a better severance package than those that pack—cold, wet, and desperate—into the later lifeboats.

Having advanced news and using it to buy a ticket into Lifeboat One is a prerequisite for the smart executive. You can be interviewed, hired, and promoted while Lifeboats Two and Three are still swinging in the corporate davits, waiting for the fog to clear.

 Knowledge is power. Stay close to decision makers and make intelligent guesses.

Being aware is everything. Bill Ayers recounts, "One of our counseling team members, before he joined us, was a senior human resources executive with a major insurance firm. He had personal responsibility for downsizing the one thousand employees under him and was well aware of the structure of the severance packages. When he saw that things weren't going to get any better in that area and would probably be trending downward, he took his opportunity, volunteered for, and accepted a package."

The moral of this story, advises Ayers, is that knowledge is power. Stay close to decision makers, make intelligent guesses as to where restructuring is heading, and couple that with an understanding of your level in the company, your age, and so on. If you reach a go decision, find out who within the organization is putting the next list together and be on it."

Advises Felipe Uria, a partner with Arco Creade, a Madrid outplacement firm, "We find that the first to leave a company that is downsizing obtains the most generous severance package." He continues, "Often companies begin downsizing by asking for volunteers and usually almost all the employees in the company are eligible to negotiate their separation. In Spain, however, this strategy is rarely used as very few people will voluntarily resign since labor legislation protects their jobs and they assume—often correctly—that by holding out the offer will be anted-up."

Stressing that the First Lifeboat theory will work in most organizations, he concludes, "The best time to get in the outplacement queue is when a company actually begins forcefully laying its employees off. If you are open to a voluntary separation, you should speak with your manager or the human resources department to let them know of your willingness to leave the company. These voluntary resignations are almost always welcomed and under the very best conditions the company has to offer."

Of course, as in everything in life, timing is all. As German outplacement consultant Herbert Muhlenhoff says, "Of course there is only a slim chance to get into a lifeboat if the captain has not ordered the evacuation of the ship." But fellow consultant Lilian Margadant in The Hague doesn't totally agree. "Just put yourself forward and start negotiations," she says. "Managers are more inclined to behave this way than other employees." In Dublin, Gerard O'Shea advises what to do until the abandon ship siren goes off, when you want to be on the first passenger list: "Watch the trends and either move toward a noncore function or move to a less solid role within the core function."

The Wrong People Go First

What all those views show of course is that it's the wrong people who go first: the people who perhaps could make a difference to an organization wallowing rudderless in a stormy sea. For whom do you need when things get rough? People with ideas, people who are prepared to take a risk, people who can come up

---

LIFE BEGINS AT FIFTY!

Writer and lecturer Tony Buzan, author of the best-selling *How to Use Your Head*, says that you shouldn't worry about losing your job when you are older because "if you are fifty and something happens you are in a similar position as when you were looking for your very first job, but with thirty years more experience."

The fact that employers tend to go for younger recruits is wrong—older people are far more intelligent. Buzan's research shows that "you actually peak physically between forty-five and fifty-five, but mentally between sixty-five and one-hundred. And another thing—the average person has his or her greatest period of success between forty-five and sixty-five."

---

with unconventional solutions. And where are they? They left in that First Lifeboat.

Observes author and lecturer Tony Buzan, "What kind of people take the first-time offer? The more courageous, the more willing to take risks, the more creative and entrepreneurial. So what many companies unwittingly do is deselect for excellence. They get the corporate equivalent of a skin disease that only lets out the good microbes and keeps the diseased (the halt and the lame) behind. And what happens if you don't treat the disease? You eventually die."

Not everyone agrees with Buzan's view, however. Some feel that among the corporations who are downsizing, there are at least some who do it right and hang on to the better people. That at least is the experience of Sally Haver, of the Ayers Group in New York, who describes a typical downsizing operation. "Usually there is a head-count mandate from senior management as to the number by which a department must be reduced by a certain time. The managers then examine their resources and will eliminate by job those that are less-than-stellar performers. This is usually done by using most recent performance evaluations," she says.

Haver continues, "There is always the employee who was not a good fit with his or her team or a scenario where a new manager is brought into an existing department and wants his or her own team. Both of these situations occasion downsizings. People who are mission-critical on a current project and are seminal to its conclusion are kept on—at least until the completion of the project." Unless of course they found a way out by volunteering to go early—

if they are that good and they see the writing on the wall they are going to do just that—which can often give people a better kick start on a new career.

This is the view taken by Daniel Leroux, a Paris-based outplacement expert, who says, "Most often the best go first, along with the least efficient. The former volunteer to enter the plan and for the others, management takes the opportunity to include them."

Leroux's experience is backed up by Eva Gotthardson, managing director of The Swedish Career Institute in Stockholm, who states her firm belief this way: "After almost seven years in this business, I am convinced that the people who are made redundant do have similarities in personality. The majority of candidates I have worked with have strong initiative and strong willpower, combined with innovativeness and the urge to try new ways. Great people in surroundings that need and appreciate these traits, but people that can hit the roof if they are put in the wrong organizational climate. My conclusion is that organizations tend to be less tolerant to strong people."

Strong people, of course, are just what you need when the organization is in a nose-dive and there is no place for Mr. Nice Guy. However, it seems that in many cases the people that should be defending the battlements have already been sent to the torture chamber of redundancy.

But there is life after death—a lot of it. Hewitt/CBC's Neil Irons believes that "becoming unemployed might just be the chance of a person's life, when the first shock has worn off. I know of a terminated forty-five-year-old manager who never went back and tried for another middle management position. He opened a sandwich bar because he loves talking and listening to people. Similarly, plant workers may discover their forgotten craft skills, an accountant might develop a hobby into a business, a manager may reconvert into a private school teacher."

Indeed if you do find yourself out there in the cold, unkind world, Tony Buzan agrees that you have got to think positive—that is the first requirement—and don't think of it as being redundant.

Irons agrees with that and adds, "The answer often lies in doing something different. The problem is to identify what that is, while taking into account not only one's technical skills but also one's interpersonal skills, personal values, and future needs as well."

In doing something different you should take time and not just rush into it all blindly. First off, it pays to think about what has happened in a positive way.

Points out Buzan, "Think about it this way. In all academic systems throughout history there has always been the sabbatical: a time for people to spend a year taking stock. Often this resulted in people changing their academic direction or initiative. So we are now being given as managers a sabbatical if you like (your severance pay is the cushion) of two or three years to be creative and get into the next stage of our career." Buzan goes on, "Now if you call that being fired or being thrown out, that is bad; but if you look at it as a paid holiday you are able to realize that you are off on a totally new life path."

> *Don't take a long vacation before starting a job search;*
> *get going from day one.*

Bill Ayers in New York agrees about the need to be positive but says it can be hard. However, he has concluded that what you have to be able to do is change the way your head sees things. And he has put together five examples.

- loss of purpose versus the reestablishment of it
- rejection versus acceptance in a new workplace
- loss of structure versus setting up of a new structure
- feelings surrounding outdated skill sets versus learning new ones
- financial concerns versus reestablishing an income stream

Whatever you do, don't go away and think about it. Sitting on a beach, hiding out up in the Alps, or just getting away from it all isn't the answer. As Gerard O'Shea, a Dublin-based outplacement consultant, warns, "In my experience, taking a long vacation before commencing the relaunch campaign is bad news. Most successful candidates start the process immediately."

Oslo-based writer and consultant Arild Lillebo takes up those issues, outlining what hard-nosed decisions you have to make, especially those that ensure that you stay positive once you find that you are, indeed, looking for a job.

"What do we say to the fifty-year-old who gets laid off after thirty years? Emotionally, this will be a terrible situation to have to face, so it may be necessary to deal with that first. My advice is find a good shoulder to cry on and then try to see things more clearly and rationally." That is part of what an effective outplacement process can do.

TWO BOUNCES AIN'T BAD

Managers from large corporations who find themselves out on the
street often end up in small and medium-sized companies and can
have a lot of trouble making the adjustment. Often they don't, and
they end up back on the street. If that happens, don't worry. Experience shows that "second bounce" executives, as they are called, have,
in fact, learned from their experience and can now bring themselves
to work without the infrastructure and support they were used to in
their initial job. As one consultant says, "Until a big company executive has been 'laundered' through one smaller company he or she
isn't any good, but it nearly always works the second time."

Lillebo goes on, "From then on, just don't give up. Even though
you have never seen a computer, never learned a foreign language,
never done anything different from running the same insignificant
office, you should know that most humans are able to adapt to new
situations. Whatever you do, don't waste your time in front of the
TV set, hanging out in the pub, or dreaming of the good old days.
Don't start drinking, don't isolate yourself."

Siding with Buzan's view of this as a sabbatical break leading to
a new start, Lillebo adds, "See this as an opportunity; a break in
your life gives you a chance to give up many bad habits and seek
new roads ahead. Take this as an opportunity to stay in shape,
physically and mentally: eat healthy foods most of the week, walk
for an hour each day; read, write, and talk to people to gain new
knowledge, new ideas, and stay mentally sound."

Lillebo continues, "Find a sensible person who can help you sort
out and clarify your alternatives. Don't turn to your buddies who
spend their days drinking in the pub or the golf club bar—they
won't be much help at all. Your old buddies will see the 'old' you—
not the 'new' you that you are about to create. Seek out and talk to
someone who is free from the picture of the 'old' you. Also, cut
your expenses and learn to live on a budget until you get some income and accept your age. It may take you time to find the new
road ahead."

If you do find yourself out on the street, having a really positive,
proactive attitude is going to get you on that new road a lot faster.
Feeling sorry for yourself or being bitter about what's happened is
going to take all the energy and focus out of your job search.

If you find yourself outside the company, you automatically—from day one—have a new job—getting a job. You must see the situation as "my job is to get another job." Being positive about it will also reflect on how you are perceived in interviews, how you sound on the phone, even how you present your resume.

Bill Ayers has identified nine plus points that make a job candidate stand out from the crowd.

- Attitude: has an upbeat, can-do attitude. Does not see him/herself as unemployable
- Gets beyond the anger and grief stage quickly; hits the ground running and starts constructive activity
- Does an immediate needs assessment between him/herself and the current jobs marketplace, evaluating honestly current skill levels and looking at what can be added to boost his/her professional attractiveness
- Open to new ideas and has a willingness to change approach if required
- A broadly focused approach: open to a variety of solutions, including interim consulting ones
- Personal charisma: a willingness to give, as well as to get, at a tough time in life. The "bread upon the waters" philosophy is alive and well!
- Constantly putting new things in the pipeline, even if practically certain he/she has a job offer in hand. Never stopping until his/her backside is in a new seat!
- A willingness to accept help
- A positive perception of his/her age and condition, whatever that may be. "We've had 'old' thirty-five-year-olds and vigorous, youthful sixty-year-olds!"

What Ayers is referring to, of course, are the lucky ones, those executives, specialists, and employees who have had the benefit of a professional shoulder to both cry on and lean on as they begin the process of getting another job.

If you think you are going to find yourself on the outside, whether you volunteer to jump or get pushed, try to make sure that you get outplacement counseling as part of the deal. Increasingly companies are using outplacement as a matter of course, but it does help to know in advance if it is available.

Indeed, many executives at their recruitment interview now insist that outplacement become part of their signing-on contract.

This ensures that there is professional help available if your assignment, for whatever reason, doesn't work out. So find out from human resources if outplacement is available in your organization. These days, you never know when you might need it.

The most important part about outplacement is that it provides a lot more than just a shoulder to cry on and a professional to help you discover that new you. It is a place to go and work each day while you carry out your job of getting a job. It provides expertise on resumes and how to conduct systematically, not haphazardly, a job search. It gives you an honest assessment of your strengths and weaknesses and can often lead you to prospect for jobs in areas you would never have thought of.

Outplacement professionals have just one task—to find jobs for their clients.

Win Nystrom, head of PCM Europe, an outplacement firm based in Brussels, and also current president of European Career Partners, a network of thirteen national outplacement companies, points out, "It's not a question any more of a CEO or an HR manager saying, 'Should I get outplacement help for the people I am making redundant?' It is a question of 'How soon in the downsizing process should I get them involved?' "

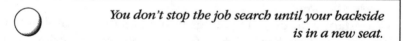

You don't stop the job search until your backside is in a new seat.

Nystrom says that the whole process, from the first rumor about job cuts to the final placement, is a progression of ups and downs (see figure "The Transitional Roller Coaster," p. 124), but there are so many plus factors in using professional outplacement counseling that it should not—for the organization's continued reputation—be regarded as a nice option but as a standard offering open to all.

For CEOs (and their HR support group), it is important to understand why outplacement is important, why it can have a positive impact on the bottom line (when spending money is perhaps the last thing you wish to do), and how it contributes to the overall image of your organization in the short, medium, and long term.

The key to understanding the ups and downs for the individual is not just reading the chart but working out where the initial damage is done and why much of it can be avoided by letting an outplacement counselor ease the period of transition early in the layoff or termination process.

FIRING YOUR CUSTOMERS!

Companies these days really need to take a responsible attitude with the people they are downsizing. That certainly is the view of consultant and business writer T.W. Kang, who heads Global Synergy Associates in Tokyo. "The company should plan the transition for the outgoing employee in an orderly and responsible manner. Nihon Digital Equipment Corporation, for example, downsized their operation by more than 10 percent using a voluntary retirement program, with rather attractive terms." Kang then adds, "The then president, Yoji Hamawaki, said he planned the program thinking of his employees as customers."

To assess any period of rapid change for the worse, we need to go back to the beginning. In this case, it is the time when the job was just about perfect. The individual was happy, enthusiastic, and motivated. Then the rumors started.

Everyone believes in rumors. It does not matter who you are, eventually you listen. Naturally you become concerned and then you worry. Then to top the rumors comes reality—termination time. Whether it is that sudden or not, the end result is shock. This is followed by a period of euphoria, a sort of mental denial, as those listed for redundancy play a mental mind game that it cannot happen to them.

Eventually, of course, it does, and after the strain of the days, weeks, or months waiting for the inevitable, the axe falling comes as a relief—albeit short-lived. This relief is quickly replaced by anger and the "I worked night and day for these people and look how they treat me" way of looking at the world. Exhausted by the anger, the typical candidate for redundancy will then try to bargain his or her way back. Rejected once more—and for the final time—the redundancy roller coaster hits rock bottom.

In case you are wondering, this is not the time you are supposed to bring in the outplacement consultant. Sadly, it is at this point that many corporations typically do.

From that lowest of the low points, the newly redundant manager recovers, begins to accept the fact that he or she is out of a job, and then sets about looking for another.

Time periods for this vary and, while there is substantial documentary evidence to support the case that outplacement gets people in new jobs faster (at all levels), let us look at some hard-nosed

The Transitional Roller Coaster.

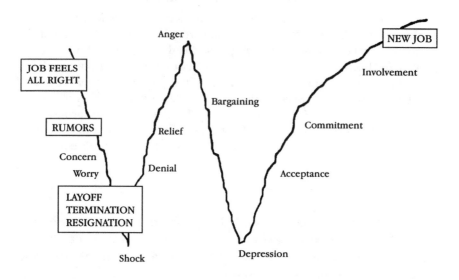

Source: PCM Europe

reasons why companies contemplating redundancy should involve an outplacement consultant at the earliest stage possible.

While accepting that there are always the little horror shows where redundancy comes like a lightning bolt straight out of the blue, scaring both management and workforce, in most cases it is planned well in advance, allowing time for rumors to build and circulate.

As we said earlier, when your former personnel are in a valley of depression is not the time to ask your friendly local outplacement consultant to call. That time is when you first contemplate the idea of reorganization, cutting out divisions, or closing down business units. So it is right at the beginning of the transition roller coaster that the outplacement consultant should be introduced. Here are five good reasons why you should bring consultants in as early as possible in the process.

- It is the right, moral thing to do. It should be part of your corporate conscience and should be consistent with the culture you are trying to foster elsewhere in the company. Would that be the view of your organization?

- It boosts internal morale, not just for those who are leaving, who see you care, but for all those left behind. If those not leaving spend half their day discussing what a poor job management is making of all this, what kind of productivity level have you got? Getting those left behind to understand why it was all necessary in the first place to keep the business going can more than pay for the cost of the outplacement process. Would your company communicate the reason in a fully professional way?
- It reduces legal vulnerability. It is better that an impending former employee spends his or her days working on getting a new job at the outplacement center than talking to his or her lawyer. Even the most misguided legal action can tie up valuable personnel and run up vast legal costs. Once again, a single action from a discontented employee can more than outweigh outplacement fees. Would your organization view it that way?
- Having an outplacement firm taking the burden leaves managers free to get on with the job of keeping the rest of the business running. Knowing their people are being looked after creates a better morale throughout the organization and means that other business decisions are made at the right time, without emotional distractions. Is that what your company would do?
- Finally, it also comes down to image. Unless you are in business for the short term, the ultimate goal of most organizations is to survive, prosper, and grow; they should be thinking that way even during a time like this. If you handle redundancy badly, you get an equally bad reputation. This means that new recruits will avoid you; banks look at you as high risk; suppliers will deal with you reluctantly. Worse still, the people left behind will begin to drift away to other jobs. Is that the way your organization would handle a redundancy process?

A bad reputation is easy to acquire. Let us consider a hypothetical manufacturing company with one thousand employees. Those employees have seven hundred spouses (not to mention girlfriends), about three hundred children old enough to understand about their parents' work, and five thousand close friends. So far six thousand people are likely to hear if something is going wrong in your little one-thousand-person company. Now add the thirty-six thousand friends and relatives of the six thousand, who know somebody who works there and so are authorities on the subject. Already we have forty-two thousand people, each briefed with a mixture of the truth, half-truths, gossip, and fiction. There are forty-two thousand potential pass-on recipients of a message for each employee (this does not add in customers and suppliers, local shopkeepers, and trade press readers).

It is to keep the value of the firm intact that outplacement should be carried out. Making outplacement available fosters a positive impression and helps individuals. To implement the outplacement process out of feelings of guilt is wrong.

So don't look at dismissal as an end. Be smart about it and think of it as a new beginning. Control it as much as you can by getting out when you, not they, choose. Of course, that's easy to say and much harder to do. But if you have your "insurance policy" fully paid up in the form of a network and guaranteed professional counseling it makes it a lot less daunting.

KEY POINTS

Note: Chapter 8 (at the back of the book) has a complete set of checklists to help you think through your future career plans. This summary is designed to help you begin to think about the issues raised in this chapter.

1. Work on your network, both professional and private: it's your lifeline for the future.

2. Do you have unfortunate delusions of entitlement to your job or organization? If you have you're a dinosaur: start thinking about the real world of today— NOT yesterday.

3. Stay aware of what's really going on and find ways to get advance intelligence: forewarned is forearmed.

4. When things get rough, don't stay around until the ship capsizes: volunteer, scratch, and bite to get in the first lifeboat. You'll be glad you did.

5. If you find yourself redundant, don't go away and think about it: your new job is getting employed.

6. Force yourself to think VERY positively: see your situation as an opportunity to seek new challenges.

What You Should Do Now . . .

1. Make a list of your frontline, secondary, and back-up networks. Who are these people and organizations? Can you really rely on them? Are they really able to support you in a time of need? These can be professional colleagues, associations, family, friends, etc. What you need to assess is, if it comes to the crunch, what will they do for you?

Key individuals and associations in my main network:

Name	*Contact*	*Assessment of their value/support*

Individuals and associations in my secondary network:

Name   *Contact*   *Assessment of their value/support*

_____

_____

_____

_____

_____

_____

_____

_____

_____

Individuals and associations in my back-up network:

Name   *Contact*   *Assessment of their value/support*

_____

_____

_____

_____

_____

_____

_____

_____

_____

Whom should I contact? Where should I go to build up/increase my network?

Go to your immediate senior manager or the human resource department and find out just what are the terms and conditions for voluntary redundancy. Are there outplacement support services available?

_____

_____

_____

_____

_____

_____

_____

_____

How to Get (re)Hired

A lot of people these days are talking about the end of the job as we know it. They are standing up in conferences and seminars and they are writing in books and magazines that the job is over, washed up, finished. There are no dead-end jobs anymore—just dead jobs, they say. In the future we won't go to work to do a job; we'll be part of a process, where we will be free to do more than the constrictions that a job description places on us. Empowerment, project work, and teamwork are in; doing your compartmentalized job is out. But as we have seen in earlier chapters there are still lots and lots of jobs—at least that's what they seem to be advertising in the want ads every week, although the jobs seem to involve much more doing and a whole lot less managing.

So what is the story? Are these people that are claiming the end of the job all wrong? Are they purveying snake oil and milking another short-lived management fad? Or perhaps they are just slightly ahead of the real-time curve.

The answer would seem to be the latter. Certainly there are lots of jobs out there, especially for executives. They might be different from before, but they definitely are individual jobs: marketing directors and managers, sales representatives, research chemists, service professionals. Sure, huge slabs of corporate middle managers have been torn from their jobs, but even they are getting jobs back. Not the same ones, but jobs all the same.

As Erik Hoffmoen of the Institutt for Karriereutvikling in Oslo said in chapter 5, "New jobs typically create a more direct content—more doing than managing, more customer contact related with greater direct accountability."

Asked if he thought the dejobbed world was just another management myth, Hoffmoen responded, "Yes, it's a myth. Of course there are jobs out there. I am putting candidates into them every day, but they are different types of jobs." He explains, "Small and medium-sized companies (SMEs) are generating the jobs, and executives and managers are getting them. Also larger companies are creating new ventures: an example of this is oil companies expanding into professional food and chain store retailing; typically the jobs generated are from external recruitment."

> *The new jobs are all about doing,*
> *not managing.*

Slooter & Partners' Lilian Margadant agrees: "The de-jobbed world is another business myth. There are jobs out there; they are just different." Staffan Kurten of HRM Partners in Helsinki also supports that view: "There are lots of jobs out there, they are just different." But then he offers an explanation for what is happening as well: "I think the confusion is that the no-specific-job issue does not yet exist on the executive level. We might be getting close to it, but employers still tend to have a rather traditional view of the employment contract. However, blue-collar attitudes are changing faster because a large portion of these people have experienced redundancies, short-term working, and so forth, so that may be why there is some confusion."

Also there is a lot more bouncing around than before, and it seems that this is a trend particularly prevalent in the United States that is set to continue. Says New York outplacement expert Bill Ayers, "In many cases the jobs out there are different, and that's because the workplace is different. Middle management has either shrunk or gone away, there are more self-directed teams, there is a more entrepreneurial feel to staff jobs, and employees are being scrutinized for value-added virtues that are much in demand in today's lean workplace. In addition, the kind of jobs that executives are getting seem to last a lot less time than any of their old ones, so that we'll see someone who was with us two years ago bounce back at the end of what turned out not to be a staff job at all—although that's what he thought he was getting—as much as a two-year project."

People who don't think that change is upon us to this great extent in Europe may have to think again. Stories and statistics of length of tenure of average executive jobs (how long people actually stay in a job position) say that they are at just the same level (seven to nine years, depending on the country) as a decade ago. The only problem with the statistics is that they only measure those who have work; they don't include all the ghosts of middle managers who aren't there anymore. So the reality could, and probably will, be different.

In this kind of environment staying aware of opportunities and watching for the next corporate tailspin are paramount. It isn't enough to get a job; you have to try to keep it or find out how best to prepare again for the exit.

In this new working world, executives certainly will have three, four, or more jobs during their careers. Instead of climbing up a vertical promotional ladder as in the past, it will be more of a snakes-and-ladders progress in different companies and different jobs. That is why we are being warned of a world without jobs. You won't own a job; you won't be known as a product manager because you probably won't always be one. And if you are it might well be for different companies, in a different industry. So there is going to be a lot of change about, and preparing for that change, making yourself employable, is going to be the number one skill. And that means knowing where to go looking.

What's Out There Job-Wise?

"What's out there job-wise?" questions Bill Ayers. He then answers, "All kinds: shirtsleeve manager jobs, all kinds of technology jobs, service sector jobs, jobs in managed health care . . . the list is endless. Fortunately, trade and consumer magazines are constantly giving us the latest hit list of what's hot and what's not." He adds, "The key is to keep your ear to the ground. If you're in a field that you want to stay in, be active in your trade and professional organizations so that you can remain on the cutting edge and know which jobs are coming up, which are down, which ones are gone forever, what companies are merging, who is expanding. Maintain your network religiously, even if you are in a secure job—of which there is absolutely no such thing these days. Above all, be diligent. With diligence, you can stay on the crest of the wave, but it takes research, work, and eternal vigilance."

Neil Irons, Managing Partner at Hewitt/CBC in Brussels, a compensation and benefits consultancy, says, "Do not think automatically of going into a profession like a lawyer or an accountant. Their halcyon days are probably drawing to a close. Also make sure you develop the right skills. Your prime education goal should be to be numerate and develop excellent interpersonal skills from the moment you know you are headed for business. For example, if you are a student, head for a summer vacation job where you can work with people, preferably in the retail trade." And he adds, "Learn to know who you are and what you want, learn to communicate. It's amazing just how many people—including university graduates—open their mouths and pour out garbage!"

> *Learn to write well.*
> *It isn't everything, but it's a lot of it.*

Dan Lund of Mori de Mexico opts for another skill he says is rare—the ability to write well. "Keep up your specialty," he advises, "but also become and maintain yourself as a person of universal culture, with obviously special areas of interest. And learn to write and write well. Writing may not be everything, but if it isn't, it's 90 percent in the long run."

Dan Lund's idea that a person needs to be rounded out, not just a technical or professional hotshot, is pursued by Spain's Felipe Uria: "I have noticed that there is a common thread among successful candidates over and above all other factors. A totally positive attitude and certain social skills. Successful candidates are not victims. They don't cry over past mistakes or get caught in the what-if? merry-go-round. They are forward-looking, focused on the positive, and proactive in the job search."

Uria adds to those attributes: "Interpersonal skills support them in the job-search process, since they will have to put all their contacts into use and will probably have to make a series of cold calls to people they don't know, who might have positions open. These skills also form part of the base of being able to interview successfully for a position."

Syntegra's Gwen Ventris says that the process for looking can be improved if hopeful candidates "really do their research, identify what the company they are chasing really needs, and tailor their offering individually to that organization."

This comment contains a key piece of advice for any job seeker: make sure you are seen as somebody THEY need and want. All too often a look through a stack of resumes yields a list of the needs

TAKING THE TRACK TO TRANSITION

With much of today's economic growth coming from small and medium-sized companies (SMEs), downsized executives from major multinationals will have to learn how to survive and prosper in a different environment where the support services and infrastructure they have grown to accept as business as usual may not be there. Making the transition from big brother corporation to fleet-footed start-up can be tough in the extreme.

Paul Unger, a vice president with A.T. Kearney Executive Search in Alexandria, Virginia, gives this advice to anyone taking the plunge from a Fortune 500 giant to an SME and becoming a career transitioner.*

Look at opportunities with enthusiasm and as a chance to tackle new challenges. For a big-company executive, it's easy to view the situation as extremely negative because it appears that his or her career has been derailed in an unanticipated way. But the successful transitioner can still reap many monetary and psychological benefits in a new environment. The sooner a transitioner accepts that corporate America is reordering its priorities and returning to smaller staffs and a more hands-on approach to dealing with services, products, and customers, the easier and more rewarding the transition will be.

Be willing to change self-perceptions. Probably the single toughest transition for outplaced executives is to change the way they perceive themselves. These executives must be willing to leave their egos in the trunks of their returned company cars. Once they accept what is, rather than reminding themselves and coworkers of what was, the new workplace can become both enjoyable and rewarding.

Acquire new skills. While everybody agrees that retraining is essential throughout one's career, it isn't a word often associated with mid- and senior-level managers. However, retraining at those levels can do much to smooth the transition after being outplaced. Acquiring new skills may be as mundane as learning how to turn on the computer and load the paper tray in the printer—and finding out where the paper is kept.

*Excerpted with permission from the June 1995 edition of *Management Review* magazine of the American Management Association.

Executive MBA programs, which are conducted primarily on weekends, can help fill in some of the skill gaps and augment existing skills. Among the classes: financial courses for nonfinancial managers, technology skills for nontechnical managers, and computer training in the use of spreadsheets and databases.

Conduct an honest self-appraisal of your management style and people skills. Get several former subordinates and peers to offer some independent and brutally forthright feedback. Executives whose styles have been imperious, dictatorial, explosive, nondecisive, uncommunicative, lethargic, politically motivated, or some combination of the above need to revamp their style to fit into the new workplace.

Be decisive. Today's environment requires involved, decisive, team-building individuals who create an atmosphere of open communication. A successful manager must involve subordinates and peers in both decision making and implementation. Smaller-company employees at all levels are encouraged and expected to take responsibility for making major decisions. Any mistake should be viewed as an opportunity to learn rather than as something to be berated. The new credo: It is better to make a bad decision than to make no decision at all.

Remember that common courtesies are essential to success. The common courtesy of returning every phone call should be moved up on the priority list. Executives should also get into the practice of writing thank-you notes and congratulatory memos on achievements. They should also recognize when a job is well done with a (figurative) pat on the back. These are all components of team building with employees, peers, and customers alike.

Decompartmentalize and broaden your view. In large organizations it is easy for executives to view their functions as entities unto themselves and to direct all their attention to those entities. But that kind of thinking constructs roadblocks, retards decision making, and establishes behaviors that might make it easier for the function but more difficult for the organization as a whole and for the customer.

Executives must view their roles in a larger context to make the transition to a smaller business. No matter what title an executive has or what his or her functional responsibilities are, everyone must focus most of their attention on making sure the customer is satisfied. If need be, all must wear multiple hats to ensure that goal is achieved.

Accept change and less security as facts of today's business life. Executives who ranked job security as a high priority in years past must realize that no company, regardless of its size, is secure. Mega mergers, acquisitions, and business unit sell-offs have caused the disappearance of some of the most visible company names in corporate history.

Small and midsize companies, where a transitioner is likely to migrate, are even more volatile and vulnerable. Mergers and acquisitions can result in significant cuts from both sides. As a result, it is prudent for executives to set career goals for themselves and devise an action plan. To maintain financial security, they should keep a minimum of six months' living expenses in liquid assets. They should also update their resumes periodically and take steps to keep current with advances in their specific field or technology.

While a lack of security may be the downside to today's corporate career, the upside is being part of a fast-paced, exciting environment in a position that offers the ability to make key decisions. Transitioners who are flexible enough to reengineer themselves successfully can thrive in a company where their impact is measurable, rewarding, and close to the action.

---

and desires of those seeking jobs. The cover letter says, "I am looking for a job as a _____ " when, if you have done your research, it should be saying, "I know you are recruiting for a _____. I am very qualified to do that job."

Here is another of those statements job seekers should cut out or copy, blow up, and hang above their desks:

Remember: Something THEY need and want:
not what YOU want.

The second point you have to get across is why they should choose you, so emphasize on any resume or in any cover letter what your achievements to date have been. As Management Centre Europe's Mike Staunton rightly emphasizes, "Get your resume together focused on what YOU have done and what YOU can DO, not your job title and your career progression since you were in grade school. The objective of a resume is to get you an interview, to get you across the desk from someone who may or may not hire you. All it is is a selling tool for YOU, so make sure it does just that."

Staunton adds, "When I look at resumes, that is all I've got to go on. In most cases I have never met the people, so what they tell me about them is important, but also how their resume relates to a job that I have open is important as well. It should sell the fact that they can do something for my organization better than the others I am considering, if I hire them."

> *Sending out masses of ill-targeted resumes is like firing a shotgun in a field at midnight in the hope of hitting a rabbit.*

Long-term human resource professionals like Staunton are convinced that in today's competitive world sending out two hundred look-alike resumes is like firing a shotgun in an open field at midnight and hoping you'll hit a rabbit—you can get very tired reloading and firing, reloading and firing, and hit nothing at all. Everyone these days says do your research and send a carefully prepared letter that addresses either the job you know is on offer or why your skills fit the products or services of their organization. And don't just mail it to the human resource director or some faceless manager (especially don't look up names in trade directories and assume the person listed will still be there)—get personal! Call the company and ask for the name of the manager you want to reach. Often sending a resume to the marketing director, the sales director, AND the human resource director can work wonders as well. As direct mail companies know only too well, you don't target a prospect company with one piece of mail—you'd quickly go out of business. You hit them with multiple pieces, to multiple people, because the chances of catching someone's interest, or even meeting a chance need, multiply dramatically that way.

Outplacement consultant Bill Ayers offers this advice: "Get together a good two-page resume, graphically good looking with enough white space so it doesn't look cramped. A summary statement, positioning YOU, that tells me why I should read on. Make it chronological rather than functional if possible with short, punchy job descriptions. Have amplified career accomplishments for each job, quantified and qualified as well. Get in there as much material that makes you stand out from the crowd (what have you done in your career that has positively impacted the bottom line of the companies you have worked for) and helps me answer the question Why should we hire you and not someone else?"

Ayers also suggests that you should test-market your resume before letting it go to work for you. "If you are in doubt about what to put in, look in current job-seeking handbooks for good examples and then pass test versions around to your friends for comments and critiques. If there is something on it that they don't understand, chances are they are not going to be the only ones. It should be a user-friendly resume, designed for the intelligent layperson, eschewing terminology particular to your form of specialization that doesn't mean anything to the outside world."

Bill Ayers also suggests that if you are one of the unlucky ones and you don't get outplacement services as part of the severance package, you may find it useful to invest in a few learning processes out of your own pocket: "If a person needs to shore up their interviewing skills, for example, it would be worthwhile to seek out and hire a private, reputable career counselor, if only for that piece of the process. Videotaped mock interviews will 'lay the truth on you' like nothing else, to help you see how you come across."

The other key that Ayers and fellow professionals keep on stressing is that it is important to do your research. Knowing the company before you get to the interview is vital. Often it can get you the interview in the first place if you show company recruiters that you already know something about their organization. "In a way you flatter them and it gives you one more advantage over the other job seekers," says one professional.

Once again it is those networks, professional and private, that can help: you hear about what's coming up and you can tap into people in those organizations and find out a lot of detail. For example, if you belong to a local chamber of commerce (most accept individual not just corporate members), a professional association, even a local sports club, they usually have a member's handbook that can be a mine of useful information and contacts. Also just picking up the phone and calling the publicity department of any reasonable-sized company usually means you can get annual reports and other published materials, free of charge. Then, of course, the Internet can provide you with open doors to many sources and professional forums, and these can also add to your knowledge and multiply your contact base. Armed with this type of

THREE THINGS TO DO RIGHT AWAY

Tom McGuire, founder and president of Clarus, a marketing communications firm based in Brussels, was a senior advertising agency executive when he decided it was time to do something on his own, so his advice about getting out—whether you or they control the process—is highly relevant.

McGuire, who realized one day during a presentation that he was making on the huge advantages of global branding (having a single name for your product everywhere) that the client he was pitching was more global than the complicated, multilabeled, multiownership mega agency he worked for, has built a global business by taking advantage of speed, technology, and continuous knowledge development.

"How all of us live and work is a process of change," he points out, "but we must recognize that there are two kinds of change: continuous and discontinuous. The latter is the most difficult to deal with because it literally catapults managers into unknown areas that directly and immediately impact how one lives."

McGuire goes on to suggest that the fifty-plus managers who suddenly, after thirty years of work, find themselves out on the street have three things they can do, whether they intend to work for themselves or another employer. Although it goes against what some seem to wish to do, anyone who really wants, or needs, a job should heed this advice.

One: Don't be frightened to move your base; in fact, if you really want to work, accept it. Too many managers won't consider this option. Explains McGuire, "Some regions of the world are growing and prospering like crazy—you can be part of that. So, my advice is, follow the sun! This could mean relocating to Silicon Valley in California, a business park in the south of France, Singapore, or Shanghai. If you limit your search to where you are right now you are cutting off thousands of leads and opportunities."

Two: Set up a multisite base of professional activity. "Keep your main residence in your home city or town, but be prepared to travel and reside temporarily in high-growth locations where you can strike new relationships and nurture employment and/or consulting activities. Managing change in your work means migrating your business contacts from capital to capital, including transcontinental moves."

Three: Buy a computer with a modem, install it, and use it. "Advances in telecommunications have made it more feasible to shrink distance and time between remote locations. Electronic transfer of files, data, and messages can be accomplished in nanoseconds—and it's cheap as well. What counts is what you deliver: your report, document, analysis, or advice. Where it was created and how it gets communicated is just not relevant. The final result governs your client's or employer's perception of added value."

In today's world, all but the most reluctant dinosaur manager can do all or any of these things; none of them are that difficult to accomplish. All of them, assuming a proactive stance and the investment in a certain portion of the redundancy package, are more than possible—they can be started today.

material you can construct a much better "cold" letter and rework your resume to fit a particular business profile.

Most of all, you must remember that there's a lot of competition out there, all looking to score a new position. If you haven't interviewed for a while and are feeling rusty and not the most attractive candidate, it might be a good idea to apply for a couple of jobs just to get the feel of what it's all about. Also, for anyone in a job, as part of that employability you want to maintain, force yourself to go out and interview for a job two or three times a year, even when you are—especially when you are—happy in your job. Knowing what questions get asked, where the emphasis is being placed, and what are the compensation packages on offer can be very reassuring. Once again it's all part of the process of being prepared.

> *Force yourself to go and interview for a job two or three times a year, when you don't need to—it's excellent practice.*

And you had better be ready, with your skills honed, because behind every downsized, middle-aged executive looking for a job, there's an enthusiastic, first-time-in-the-market college graduate who will do anything for a job. And he or she doesn't go about getting a job like mum and dad did. Oh no, he or she is committed and ruthless.

A report from the Arbor Group, a human resource consultancy based in New York, reveals that today's young job seekers would rather write a letter to a short list of companies they have targeted, explaining the challenges they know these firms are facing and how they can be part of the solution, than write a letter to a long, unfocused list of companies. Most important, they report, before these young people write letters, they become walking encyclopedias about the companies they are focusing on. They research every source of information—the Internet, Nexis, Compuserve, America OnLine, Dow Jones, and so on—until they know each organization's past, present, and future.

Once those letters are in the mail, that isn't the end of the story. They don't wait around for the mail carrier! The young and relentless, as the Arbor Group have christened them, won't give up until they have made contact with the person they've written to. They will cold call, fax, and e-mail until they get attention.

Asked what is the ultimate secret for these people, the Arbor Group reports that networking is the key. These young job seekers won't even go to the laundromat without a business card tucked in the back pocket of their jeans.

That view is backed up by Sally Haver of the Ayers Group, also headquartered in New York, who lays out this advice: "Use every arrow in your quiver. Network. Write targeted campaign letters, talk to recruiters, answer advertisements. Join community and church groups dedicated to helping job seekers. Tell everyone—and I mean everyone—that you are looking for a job; offers can appear from the most unlikely places. Also let your network know who you are, where you've been, what you've done, what you have to offer, and the kinds of places that can put it to good use."

Who's Getting Hired and Why?

And what are those recruiting looking for? What do they want in today's tough business world—this new world of work? Equally, what don't they want to see? An understanding of what makes a candidate attractive and how to enhance the skills people need is going to be essential to getting another job.

Managing partner of executive search firm Heidrick & Struggles' Brussels office, Baldwin Klep says that there are three key attributes that successful candidates need to have or at least convince the prospective employer they have.

- A track record of creating change: "Every company needs to change constantly to keep up with new developments in an increasingly transparent and competitive business environment. Candidates for my clients need to have done it before; they need to demonstrate that they have the courage to break through the safe status quo and tackle things on a project-oriented basis."

- A team builder: "Not only to motivate the stable team of direct reports but also to have the ability to spot the right individuals in the organization to come together, effectively, on a project basis."
- Cultural mobility: "The mental ability to be comfortable dealing with other nationalities and with other business situations. Key to this is to have the ability to be objective about the situation of one's own country in the context of the European and wider international scene."

Klep has three negatives to add to his list. Prospective candidates should note these as well—turnoffs can kill even the best candidate.

- Talking too much: "If you are talking too much you are not listening and thus not appreciating the real issues in a conversation."
- Looking for guarantees: "There are no certainties or guarantees in a world of constant change. Executives have to take risks in terms of both organizational structure, with often difficult to measure matrix responsibilities, and personal risks that their performance will be good enough to be rewarded in today's balance between base and variable compensation."
- A soft handshake!: "The first, ominous signal of an individual without courage and determination."

That soft handshake isn't just one man's turnoff either! It has been cited by executive search consultants in the United States, Sweden, Spain, France, and Singapore as a major turnoff. So don't just check out your resume with your friends; practice a strong, assertive handshake with them as well.

 Practice a firm handshake; soft ones won't get you hired!

The other thing that can turn off both professional recruiters and their clients is the job hopper. There is also a point where staying too long is viewed with suspicion as well. Explains Andrea Wine of executive search firm Tasa, based in Brussels, "Job hopping shows a lack of career coherence, although staying in the same position doesn't necessarily demonstrate career coherence either. Someone who has stayed seven years in the same position should have a se-

WORLD TRAVEL—WHO WANTS IT?

There's a lot of advice being thrown around about being prepared to relocate, but be careful; when it comes to the crunch, it just may not be for you. A wandering expatriate warns, "Never forget if you get into the 'I'm available to travel anytime anywhere group,' that's just what can happen to you. You can be on hold, waiting to move for months before it happens and then be expected to pack up in a week and get yourself and the family halfway around the world. That's the reality.

"Worse still, the people who actually do this seem to take endless grief from their stay-at-home colleagues about how someone else 'should have' or 'almost had' or was a 'leading candidate' and really should have been the person to go instead of you. What never gets said is that when it comes down to packing up your stuff and moving halfway around the planet, most people seem to find a last-minute, compelling reason why they can't do it."

Advice: Check out what you and your family REALLY think about this idea before, not after, you relocate.

rious question mark after them: What have they gained after their first four years in the position? That is, unless there is a very clear reason and it can be seen as part of their career plan."

So there is a definite time span when—unless you have the best of excuses—if you haven't received that new assignment, position, or even promotion, you had better decide it's time to grab the passing parachute and jump for it, if only to preserve the long-term good of your career.

Another turnoff that is more common than many would suspect is arrogance. Observes Wine, "Some people are surprised to discover that they come across as arrogant. This can often be the case with people who have had success quickly in a company, someone who has moved up rapidly—the highfliers."

I suspect that there is an invisible sign hanging in every interview room around the world—Job-hopping, arrogant executives with limp handshakes need not apply!

There's something else that I suspect may have something to do with cultural differences; in Europe (in some places) it is not good to mention money too early in the interview process.

Comments Neumann International's Gerhard Krassnig from Vienna, "Candidates should not mention the financial aspects, the salary in the first interview. It is bad form. Also, self-confidence and not arrogance is important. They should also be a good listener, not taking more than 50 percent of the time to talk about themselves and remember to pose questions that show you are well prepared."

Fellow Neumann consultant Carlos Cortes from Madrid warns that you shouldn't just plunge into a job, even if you get an offer. "Be prudent when considering a change of company," he advises, "insist on meeting and pay very close attention to the team that you would be joining."

Cortes' point is very important. Faced with redundancy it is easy to feel a tremendous euphoria if you are offered a job. But it is important to think it through. Is it the right group? What are the prospects? Will I fit in?

One other issue that might be helpful to keep in mind is that executive search consultants don't like unsolicited resumes popping through their mail slots. To a man and woman they all said that this was not the way for an executive looking for a job to get very far. They put the resume on file, but they say that fewer than 10 percent of all successful search assignments are filled from people who just mailed in their resume. Basically these people just got lucky. Indeed, an executive search office can be the source of more economic indicators than just about anywhere else. Any rumor of a potential downsizing in a major corporation has resumes fluttering like autumn leaves on the desks of headhunters well in advance of any official announcement.

The best way to meet face-to-face with headhunters is long before you need them to help you. In fact the best advice is get to know three or four personally, through industry or trade associations or your fitness or sports club. Once again it is building and using that personal network that counts. There is no point trying to see a search consultant when you are out of work, but there is a lot of use getting to know one when you are gainfully employed. And don't forget either that they may just have a better position for you in the bargain.

Years ago I was sitting in a meeting with a senior vice president of a major U.S. corporation. We were in a heavy, long negotiation and his phone rang; he had told his secretary to hold all calls. It was a headhunter, and he talked for three or four minutes. When the call was over, the senior vice president said, "Sorry about that, but now he owes me a favor and you never know when I'll need him. Here's a tip, never turn down a call from a headhunter. It's a useful life insurance."

Where Are You on the Ladder of Life?   .

The other thing that needs consideration is just where are you on the ladder of life? As we heard earlier and as we have already seen in outplacement examples, you might not want to go back into a full-time high-stress position. If you are over forty-five, with some savings and a good severance package, you might be able to consider something that really interests you, that is different, or something that gives you time to pursue other interests. Like the Spanish executive described in chapter 5, who realized that he could take a 30 percent pay cut because he could afford it and his children were no longer a financial consideration, you could find a job that has a high level of satisfaction in an area you have never previously considered.

One of the major motivations for people changing the way they look at things is part of that point raised by author and lecturer Tony Buzan: people have the time to consider what they want to do. While many of us will not have the luxury of sitting around and thinking about the real values we want to get out of the rest of our lives, many can do just that.

According to data available in the United States from outplacement organizations, many downsized executives—especially those over forty-five—just don't want to move. Career Counselors International, a network of outplacement consultancies across the United States, reports that "eighty-five percent of downsized executives won't move. They will take less money, and they will happily take a year to find something in their home area, but they won't move."

Career Counselors International believes there are three compelling reasons for this attitude.

- There are no guarantees of security anymore. Even if they move, in two or three years they may find themselves downsized again in a place they have only just got to know. Therefore, it is better to stay where your family and friends are.
- The quality of life issue is paramount. If they have paid off their house and seen the kids through college, why not wait and get a job locally—even if it is lower paid—and enjoy life a little more?
- The double career issue. People will move for their first job but then the dual career kicks in, so often one won't move if the other doesn't want to. Also, picking up on what Buzan suggested,

---

NO TO CAREER MANAGEMENT

Despite rumors to the contrary, it looks exceedingly unlikely that executive recruiters will take on responsibility for the careers of a stable of top-notch senior executives, as is already common in sports and entertainment. Citing the conflict that would arise between their traditional client (the company) if they started peddling talent to the highest bidder, no headhunter interviewed saw this as a wave of the future. However, the recent move by some search firms into what they term management contracting would seem to herald something of the sort, albeit dressed in a different guise; except that, again, the client is supposed to be the company not the individual. If truth be told there will never be any great incentive to represent individuals at the expense of clients; there just isn't the same amount of fee income available.

---

if one partner is still in full-time work, they are possibly able to afford not going back to work—ever.

So for a large group of people, the urgency, the need, the drive isn't all that important as it may have been a generation, even twenty years ago. Inheritance from parents and severance or early retirement packages have changed the rules and our perceptions considerably. As one career counselor says, "For many people, after forty-five or so, the real fear is not that of failing to get a job; it is the fear of leaving the place you have put down roots. There is no doubt that a lot of people are capable of putting up with—even enjoying—lesser paid jobs and jobs with little or no responsibility. This is just as true of a lot of senior executives who already made it and are looking for something different now as middle managers who decided that they are not going to jump back in the rat race again."

Additionally, there are others who are selling up in cities with high real estate price tags and taking the leap to a new life of leisure or semileisure by buying in a cheaper market.

This rejection of jobs at any price is not just a U.S. trend. Outplacement consultants in Europe also report a similar response in those who, having assessed themselves honestly, are able to look with a fresh mind at the next stage of their life.

Herbert Muhlenhoff in Dusseldorf says, "It is a question of quality of life; some today accept relocation, others do not." That view is amply supported by Erik Hoffmoen in Oslo, who finds that "it all has to do with the economic circumstances of the executive and the size of the payoff package. If there is little chance that the bailiffs are going to be knocking on the door in the near future it is tempting—and psychologically right—for the executive to adopt a clean sheet approach. The theoretical opportunities are unlimited, and it is a time to examine yourself and your own needs as well as what unlimited choice means in reality."

In the United Kingdom and Ireland it's the same trend. Consultants tracking ex-managers all report an unwillingness to pull up the tent and head off to another location. "There has been a big change in this last five years," says one. "Career has definitely taken a sec-

---

WHAT'S YOUR MANTRA?

In interviews for this book I asked people to tell me their personal philosophy for getting through the business day. What did they believe in? What was the mantra they could say each morning as they shaved or brushed their hair? Remarkably, all were soft thoughts rather than tough, competitive phrases that one might have expected from people who all populate a hard world of work.

Here are some of the responses—all different and all relevant in their own way—and the respondent's reasons for believing in them.

Stay ahead of others; stay ahead of yourself. Everything is as it should be, but not for you. Keep moving.
        —Don Bates, Sumner Rider & Associates, New York

Take a chance, take and risk and make the most of your opportunities. You don't know what your potential is until you find out.
        —Linda Holbeche, Roffey Park Management Institute, UK

I don't have a personal rule, but I think that people should have a positive mind and seek to gain enjoyment from what they do. I think it is very unhealthy for individuals to experience dissonance with work. An unhappy and unfulfilling work life can be a life sickness.
        —Glen Petersen, Lion Nathan, New Zealand

Never, never stop learning. Stay flexible and get to know as many people as you possibly can. The relationships that you build throughout your life will be your lifeline to the future.
        —John Doerr, Management Centre Europe, Brussels

> *Every day my contribution has to add value to the organization I work for. The most difficult thing is to respond to a customer's needs and keep them happy. Remember that customers are always right, but they are not always reasonable!*
> —Sultan Kermally, Economist Conference Unit, London
>
> *Where's my next purchase order coming from?*
> —Tom McGuire, Clarus, Brussels
>
> *There is a saying in Asia: "If you cannot win by pushing, try pulling." In a professional service like consulting—even if you come across what you think is a legitimate need for a client—you can push and push and there will be no acceptance by the prospect. At other times, clients will come to you with what they think is a need and engage you, only to discover that the real need is very different from what they thought. Therefore, one has to be very flexible from a timing standpoint. If you push all the time you will get burnt out very quickly.*
> —T.W. Kang, Global Synergy Associates, Tokyo

ond position if redundancy happens after fifty. They just won't sell their house; they'll consider commuting, but they won't sell."

Writer and consultant John Humble observes this trend even among middle managers, who he believes are often just as likely to stay put as the better-off ex-executive. His observations are remarkably similar to those of the Career Counselors International group in the United States. "Relatively young highfliers—the managers who have lost their job but have a bit of capital and a bit of spare time to find the right position are the most likely candidates for staying put," he says. "For the great mass of middle managers, moving one's home is a tough and invariably impossible step."

Humble cites reasons very similar to the U.S. experience.

- A house move usually involves costs, at a time when they are financially weak.
- The two partners' work pattern is well established. Moving means that the still working partner inevitably loses his or her job.
- "Home" means access to backup. There is an established local fabric of friends, relatives, and children.

- It is perceived by middle managers as a high-risk solution (just like the U.S. experience). Surveys show that even after getting a job middle managers especially worry if this new job will be any safer than the last. So is it worth the giant step of moving at all?
- Where people do take jobs that take them away from home all week the pressures on home life that are created are not all that encouraging.

For those others, the younger managers who are still in demand, their unwillingness to disrupt their close family life and give up a long-term association with a place is different, but it is not stopping them from getting jobs. And they are willing to commute. The old IBM acronym—I've Been Moved—doesn't work anymore, but it is being adapted, just as we are all adapting to new roles and new realities. However, it does seem from the evidence so far that quality of life is paramount and is most certainly a new trend that recruiters and employers alike are going to have to deal with.

At the other end, things are changing as well. Highfliers are demanding and getting a new work cycle that is different from before. What highfliers—especially where they really are a catch for a company—are saying is, "If you want me, this is where I live and I'm not relocating. I don't mind coming to the office Monday through Friday, but I'm going to commute home on weekends. Anyway, as I spend a lot of time on planes and as I am always in touch by e-mail, I don't need to be in your city 365 days a year."

In Europe, where commuting has been traditionally inside countries, this is creating a whole new tribe of executive gypsies, who climb on and off planes on Fridays and Mondays, cut deals with airlines for special ticket fares, and still manage to stay sane and employable.

Others think that moving to where the new jobs are is still the best option. Certainly, if you are just starting out it makes good sound sense. Says Glen Petersen of New Zealand beverage group Lion Nathan, "Yeah, moving's a good idea! If industry and opportunity have the tendency to move in geographic ways, then I guess the workforce needs to adopt that same capability. If the choices are stay put and be a victim or move and continue to prosper, then I know which one I'm going to take."

Brussels-based publisher David Starr agrees: "I have no difficulty with the concept of people moving to find work. This is a time-honored tradition, and we must not look at work, people, and regions as static. The problem is that governments have established artificial barriers to the free movement of people and work."

Starr's comment is the final piece in the finding-work puzzle. Assuming that you are not content to sit and watch the roses grow—a dangerous scenario to adopt unless you are really well padded against what the future can throw at you—you cannot begin to look at the workplace the way it used to be. Apart from the United States and possibly Japan, where it is possible to move within the nation state to find work, many other countries can't provide that luxury anymore. And with economic woes still plaguing Europe very few executives—certainly few under forty — will have the luxury of refusing to move. So Asia, for example, must be considered a viable employment option for those cast aside in European industry shakeouts.

Here is the dichotomy. There is one group of enthusiastic, up-to-the-minute executives who will tell you it doesn't matter where you work anymore because we are all citizens of cyberspace. However, there is an equal group that will tell you that if you want to be plugged into the real world, if you want to be able to meet lots of people, get to interviews easily, and keep up to date in a personal (rather than an impersonal) fashion, you had better be somewhere you can meet people face to face.

Possibly the answer, apart from a few loners who certainly would never have made managers in any incarnation, is somewhere in the middle. Just as stars hate Hollywood and live in the mountains but cannot afford to miss the Oscar ceremony or seeing their agents, so we must be plugged in at all times. The phone, fax, and Internet are handy helpers, but they will take us only so far in our networking needs.

> *We need to spend at least some time physically where the work is given out.*

And this means that whether we are trying to get a job, set up our own business, or create a part-time niche, we need to be, sometimes at least, physically in the place where the work is given out. For the moment, no matter what anyone says, that means getting together with the movers and the shakers in the business you want to succeed in.

Another thing to watch for from a business point of view is that countries are ceasing to matter and places are assuming a greater importance. Places are where things happen; they are concentrations of people and opportunity. As we said earlier, you are more likely to find a job in New York than in the middle of Kansas. Equally, you are more likely to get a professional's job or a manager's job in Paris than in Pau, in Barcelona than in Badajoz. All right, you may be able to plug into the World Wide Web and surf the globe. You may be able to "talk" to others and share ideas. But when it comes to doing business, people like to see the other person.

If you are a specialist, yes, you can live in a cottage on an island off the coast of Norway part of the time. But you'll have to go to Oslo three or four times a year to keep your contacts up, buy them

---

ADVICE TO AN EIGHTEEN-YEAR-OLD

If you are an eighteen-year-old, a precocious twelve-year-old, or a late-starting twenty-one-year-old, this section applies specifically to you. The idea is simple. Here are some things should you be doing now to make yourself more employable than your colleagues when you leave school, college, or other further education.

Some are predictable.

- Work during vacations for a business and get as much experience as possible.
- Learn languages and culture. If English is not your first language, make sure it is a very close second.
- Make sure you are thoroughly computer literate.
- Learn the softer interpersonal skills and practice them.
- Join clubs and associations and begin to create a lifelong network.

And then do what Don Bates advises. "Distinguish yourself from the herd, go the extra step, stay the extra hour, show the extra initiative."

Outplacement executive Bill Ayers has seven points that make a really good set of needs that you can work on and are designed so you'll get practice in:

- delivering what your employer really wants
- just plain showing up on time and being reliable. That counts for more than you know
- being part of the solution rather than being part of the problem, which is your best attitude lesson
- seeing how things work in the real, for-profit world
- learning basic business and office procedures
- learning the hard and soft skills that make you a good candidate for your next job, such as learning to be a good team player,

acquiring good work communication skills, learning to tolerate work styles different from your own, learning new computer software for the business world

- basic business math, basic physical inventory of what's needed in the workplace, what things cost, how executives make decisions on how company money is spent.

"Finally," says Ayres, "I would encourage eighteen-year-olds to try to find work in a place large enough so that they can pick out and watch someone who could be a role model, and then emulate the person. It helps to develop a steep learning curve."

Then there is a slightly slower, more considered way suggested by Dan Lund in Mexico City, who wholeheartedly agrees with Bill Ayers but concludes, "Summers might be best spent swimming, hiking, and falling in love—internships can come later. Young people should not deny either political interests or artistic effort, even if it seems a bit of a life detour. With enough red wine, life is longer than most young people anticipate!"

a beer, and say hello. If you are really specialized you'll have to take a plane to meet your virtual colleagues wherever they are, wherever the work comes from.

Watch out for teleworking. No one's quite sure yet where it is going or remotely certain where it will all end up. You might get a job, as a software programmer, say, and be given all you need. Upload every morning and download every night. But if you are not in the center of things, where it all happens, where real people interact, how can you keep up to date or know the shifting sands of the corporate political climate? How do you find out about those upcoming corporate reorganizations, for instance? Sooner or later you will lose out—BIG!

So take care with your search for a job. Start it as quickly as you can, progress as fast as you can, get focused, and convince that face-to-face network to go the extra mile for you. If you have the luxury of not having to do it all over again and really can work part time, great. Just make sure you have really assessed your position. You don't want to be looking for work in ten years' time, do you?

Finally, don't think cyberspace will solve anyone's problems. It will bring those places in the world where the action happens closer together, but we will still need that feel of sharing ideas, successes, and, yes, failures as well.

Above all, do what's right for you and you alone. If you think what someone is telling you is bad advice, ignore it and do it your way. Remember, in the new work phrase, you are in charge of yourself! Everyone is different. That's what makes finding what is right for us such a challenge and a totally unique experience.

KEY POINTS

Note: Chapter 8 (at the back of the book) has a complete set of checklists to help you think through your future career plans. This summary is designed to help you begin to think about the issues raised in the chapter.

1. New jobs for the new working world are all about doing, not telling. Make sure you get these skills. They are the passport to employability.

2. People get interviews because they create interest, because they INDIVIDUALLY target each company and learn about it.

3. Remember: It's something THEY need—not what YOU want—that counts.

4. Limp handshakes are out! Be confident, and, like your handshake—FIRM.

5. Telework—living life at the other end of a modem—is not a 100 percent solution: no one can exist in isolation and stay in work. Remember the network.

What Should You Do Now?

1. Assess just what doable things you can do and where you are really just an old-fashioned manager (a teller of tasks, an organizer, not a player in the work). Find out which areas you need to improve on or learn from scratch.

Things about my job/profession I do well:

_____
_____
_____
_____
_____
_____
_____
_____

Things about my job/profession I need to work on and improve:

_____
_____
_____

_____
_____
_____
_____
_____
_____

Things about my job/profession I need to learn/relearn:

_____
_____
_____
_____
_____
_____
_____
_____
_____

2. Make a list of the attributes YOU have that others need. Remember NOT
    what you need—what THEY need: what will interest them about YOU.

Key attributes I can offer a company and why

Key attribute   *Why it's important*

_____
_____
_____
_____
_____
_____
_____
_____

So You Want to Go It Alone?

Entrepreneurs are risk-takers, willing to roll the dice with their money or reputations on the line in support of an idea or an enterprise. They willingly assume responsibility for the success or failure of a venture and are answerable for all its facets. The buck not only stops at their desks it starts there too.

—VICTOR KIAM

The reason a lot of people do not recognize opportunity is because it usually goes around wearing overalls and looking like hard work.

—THOMAS EDISON

In the preceding chapters of this book there have been references to the third alternative for executives who find themselves made redundant: going it alone. To review, the other two are getting a job with another company and leaving full-time work to retire early or do a little part-time work.

There are lots of views about going on your own. Some experts say that it is a choice that few people can ever make a real success out of because they are just not geared to it. Others point out that since there is a trend to be more self-reliant in the future—even inside organizations—we are all going to have to live like that so we had better learn these skills anyway.

In addition, there are also several myths about going it alone that confuse the picture. The first is that many downsized executives opt for this choice—in reality few do. The second myth is that there are thousands of happy self-employed former middle managers raking in fortunes—in reality there may be a lot of publicity for the ones that are doing well, but they are by no means an army.

The truth is that choosing to go it alone can be a lot of hard work, not to mention heartache. But, if you find yourself out on the street, it should be regarded as one of the options that you might want to consider—but consider it carefully indeed.

In the view of the career counseling professionals who deal with the Shall I open my own business? question every day, fewer people choose that option than people would imagine. However, the counselors also admit that it is a good idea to discuss this during the outplacement process with your consultant or examine it thoroughly with others—especially your spouse and family.

It also depends greatly where you are in your career and how successful you have been to date. For example, if you are a highflier middle manager under forty years old who got downsized in some unexpected reshuffle, you would probably steer clear of the go-it-alone option, unless your network was particularly good. On the other hand, if you are heading toward fifty years old and have fewer financial responsibilities and are frankly a little tired of the organizational life, self-employment might appeal to you a lot more.

What you have to realize is that doing it halfway, thinking you can putter about at something you like, usually has disastrous consequences for all but the luckiest. Like all things, you either do it wholeheartedly or not at all, and it does take a lot of hard work not just initially but to keep the business going.

Says Margaret Newborg, an outplacement consultant in New York, "with people over forty-five years old, most consider, at least initially, going into an entrepreneurial role. We don't prevent this, of course, but it is also up to us to open up alternative career paths, so that if their idea doesn't work out they are not disillusioned."

 Don't put your savings or severance pay into something unless you know you'll be good at it.

Gerard O'Shea from Dublin takes a stronger view: "A good 25 percent of our outplacement candidates get the idea of setting up their own business, but most are just not suited. In fact one of the things we do is try to dissuade them from this, particularly in putting their severance pay or savings into something they, frankly, are not going to be good at." However, O'Shea puts this into context when he adds, "We encourage our candidates to view themselves as products with a range of skills that a customer may wish to buy. Obviously some organizations may want them for short-term assignments and candidates are encouraged to consider this option."

French outplacement expert Daniel Leroux surmises that there "will probably be more people in charge of their own employment, self-employed, employed by several organizations at the same time,

---

BEING PRESENTABLE IN MORE WAYS THAN ONE

If you do decide that you have the skills—however deeply buried—to go it alone, you cannot do without the ability and confidence to present well, to become a smooth, persuasive, but credible marketer. My advice is don't neglect this side of your abilities; if you don't like people, don't like selling to them, don't like standing up in front of a group and talking, either get to like it or don't take the plunge. Remember, doctors that succeed have a good bedside manner; self-employed accountants have more than just numbers in their quiver of skill arrows.

Equally, make sure that you not only present your ideas well but that you also present yourself well. Don't make sales calls in jeans unless you are a tree surgeon or running a pizza franchise. Think seriously about your personal presentation—the way you look. Ask yourself that old saw, "Would you buy a used car from this person?" It may sound trite, but first impressions really DO count.

---

or working within a network; however, the great majority will certainly remain classical salary earners."

Leroux explains that going it alone is "not an easy move as most people are not equipped to face uncertainty, stress, and other risks. As an outplacement consultant I therefore hesitate to encourage such a dramatic move. Indeed, most of the time we actually examine with candidates why they should not follow that option."

German candidates seem to reflect the overall European hesitation with self-employment as well. Reports Herbert Muhlenhoff from Dusseldorf, "Apart from a few exceptions, our clients have shown little enthusiasm for being self-employed. It appears that for as long as they can they would prefer to stay within a company and only when all other avenues have been exhausted would other activities be considered. Maintaining the standard of living, responsibility for the family, status within your circle of acquaintances, and the level of personal risk seem to be the major factors against self-employment."

Muhlenhoff adds another point: "We also feel that Germany—compared to other parts of Europe and certainly the United States—is behind in the development of executives becoming service providers, that is, working for more than one organization at a time. Reasons for this seem to be that unemployment benefits are relatively generous and postpone the need for real change. Also, many unemployed are simply not the active types who would take the initiative."

Frank Ebbinge in The Hague agrees with Muhlenhoff and points out that "in our experience an estimated 15 percent of people become providers to a range of corporations. Most people find it too frightening and opt for security."

But while it is estimated that less than 5 percent of Europe's management workforce is earning a living as a service provider to a range of corporations, the trend is further along in the United States. As Bill Ayers in New York comments, "Realistically, about a third or more of our candidates, realizing that consulting—in one form or another—is truly the wave of the future, are preparing for this, either by setting up their own consulting firms or by looking for and accepting project assignments with consulting firms or client companies."

So it would seem that this trend is going to take place over the next five to ten years, particularly as most new work ideas eventually migrate—albeit with some modifications—from west (the United States) to the east (Europe). However, the points raised by the European outplacement consultants are valid and may well account for the reasons why the United States is getting people back to work faster. Lacking Europe's social security safety net, out-of-work managers are getting themselves back into jobs or building a portfolio of clients because they have no other option. Conversely, in Europe, executives who may have both a generous severance package—three or four years' salary is not uncommon—plus the social security cushion can take their time to look for what they want. They didn't join the swollen ranks of "instant consultants" because they had no pressing need to do so.

Portfolio management—where an executive has a group of organizations as his or her clients rather than a single, full-time job— is not being viewed with enthusiasm by everyone. Indeed, there is a strong feeling that portfolio management—it already has a negative buzzword aura about it—is seen in some quarters as a serious destabilizer of many management careers.

As consultant and writer John Humble explains angrily, "I think that most of the stuff being written and talked about on the subject is not only wrong but also cruel. Just think about it seriously for a moment: How many managers really have the outstanding competence to sell themselves to a number of different firms? And those firms may be in different types of work, in different industries. I don't think that, in the long run, firms are going to be all that keen on such people anyway."

He goes on, "The majority of middle-aged, middle-ranking managers have knowledge and skills that are—by the way their work was structured—narrowly specific." Giving examples, he goes on, "The engineer who used to run maintenance for analog telephone exchanges, the purchasing manager for concrete garden ornaments—their chances of building a portfolio of clients are frankly zero."

But, on the upside, he explains, "Those with outstanding general professional knowledge and skills—personnel managers, accountants, marketing and selling executives—are the best placed to build a portfolio. And I use the word 'outstanding' deliberately—clients are not willing to pay for mediocrity."

Humble, echoing the thoughts of others, says that there are four attributes that anyone embarking on an entrepreneurial or portfolio management route had better have a great deal of:

- the ability to sell themselves
- the ability to manage the complex logistical tasks that go with servicing multiple clients who ALL want first priority and all wanted it yesterday
- the psychological strength to work alone, taking total personal responsibility for finding work, delivering excellent service, and looking after the administration and finances
- the willingness to sacrifice some short-term earnings to invest time in keeping state of the art in their professions

Humble should have added one more: the motivation and good health to work on into the night, during holidays and weekends. Self-motivation is probably the key to working alone.

Humble adds, "By the way, many managers looking for employment like to call themselves consultants. Changing the title sadly does not change the problem. I have a lot of firsthand experience of even very senior managers, excellent performers in every respect, who have lost their jobs and tried the portfolio route with total failure. Disguising the process of looking for a job as a consultancy is a commonplace ploy, but the problem remains the same."

Humble continues his argument this way: "To be a so-called portfolio manager will be a logistical and organizational nightmare for those not properly equipped. They won't be able to juggle even the smallest portfolio. I don't understand this move at all; we know only too well that most people only work well in teams and become totally demotivated when working alone."

Humble has hit on one important item that does not seem to be given much of an airing in all these grand schemes of the new working world. Certainly we can agree that the job has changed. It hasn't gone away; it is different. We are having to get used to teamwork and being T-form managers with a broader skill set than just our professional and technical training can give us. Equally, the new working world demands that we take charge of our careers because no one else is going to do it for us. What going it alone also does is remove the security that comes even with the new-style job and saying that even that will eventually be under threat.

Unless you have the head, the heart, and the energy for it, portfolio management, independent consulting, call it what you will, isn't going to get a big vote from those newly redundant executives looking for a job.

Entrepreneurial versus Self-Managed

In fact Humble's abhorrence and concern can be summed up in a way that most people haven't bothered to examine: there is a major distinction between being entrepreneurial and being self-managed.

 Don't confuse entrepreneurism with self-management.
We can all be self-aware and self-reliant.

Self-managed (what we all have to be in the new working world) is taking responsibility for ourselves and our career: it means self-awareness and self-reliance. It by no means suggests self-employment.

Entrepreneurial means doing it yourself, making it yourself, and serving it yourself. You can be entrepreneurial inside an organization, but then they call it intrapreneurial, which is a different thing altogether. Self-managed is taking care of YOU. You don't have to be entrepreneurial to do that right.

So, make quite certain that you understand BEFORE you take any plunge and start a multiclient workload. Whatever anyone says to you, whatever articles you read, you had better be an entrepreneur and have a true entrepreneurial view of the world if you are going to go that way. All those outplacement consultants who are giving frank, expert advice are doing exactly the right thing when they say, "OK, think about it, but unless you are very, very sure, don't do it."

And that is my advice too. Unless you really feel you can sell yourself, sell your product, sell your service, not just once or twice but every day; unless you feel that you can be your own finance director, strategic planner, human resource manager, marketer, and the rest, don't even attempt it. Many have, and many have come to grief over doing so.

Here's Tom McGuire of marketing communications firm Clarus— who founded the business himself—talking about his experiences: "Entrepreneurism takes nerves of steel. It means worrying day and night where your next billable project or sales order will come from. To be a successful entrepreneur means taking risks and shouldering responsibilities that workaday employees never dream of. For example, entrepreneurs must constantly worry about making their payroll month after month."

So if you don't like that sort of life, once described as a permanent bungee jump, what else can you do? McGuire has some suggestions: "For those who are neither emotionally nor mentally equipped to act as an entrepreneur, there are three routes to pursue.

"First, find an alternative. This means working, say, as a contract employee or independent consultant, WITH [note this] the security of a contract. It relieves you from worrying about making monthly payroll, building employee motivation, covering overhead, and ensuring sufficient working capital to start up and sustain your entrepreneurial enterprise.

"Second, you can try to engage in a trial passage from employee to independent entrepreneur. This means establishing a twelve-month business plan, which anticipates worst and best scenarios: worst is financial failure, best is financial success and independence. To organize your trial passage is not easy; it means having sufficient funds to support your activity during one year, even in the worst case.

"Finally, if you are not disposed to becoming an entrepreneur, you can always try seeking a partner who shares your risk and uncertainty. One-plus-one can equal three in delicate and dangerous phases of creating and continuing your own business."

In case you are getting really enthusiastic about all this entrepreneurial hype, McGuire has a cold shower of words for you:

THE CHANGING JOB PERCEPTION

One problem that many executives (particularly those in Europe) have is that when they lose their job they are reluctant, usually because of pride and peer recognition, to take a position that may appear menial or is not perceived as being an executive or managerial role. However, with downsizing so common these days much of that is beginning to change.

As Karen Schele, a consultant with the Svenska Management Gruppen in Stockholm, recounts, "Even in Sweden I can see a changed outlook today with people who have had high-prestige jobs accepting those that they might have found more menial. For example, the other day a friend of mine asked what my neighbors did for a living. I told her that they were now both employed by the local authorities and looked after old people in their homes during the weekends and that Mrs. X was also an artist who paints icons and her husband is a freelance masseur. Five years ago my friend would almost certainly have said, 'So they don't have real jobs do they?' Now she thought it was very good what they were doing. I think if you have the mentality for this that it is an excellent solution. You have steady income—even if it is not enormous—and you get to do things you really want and enjoy doing."

"The hallmark of every successful entrepreneur is that he or she worries relentlessly not only about starting up but also surviving in the long run. To do so you must be ready to work long and hard: evenings, weekends, and holidays. The minute you stop pedaling is the moment you start falling behind. There is always somebody out there able to work harder and smarter than you."

Linda Holbeche, director of research at Roffey Park Management Institute in the United Kingdom, reckons that a lot of the success of the entrepreneur is bound up in indefinable factors like judgment. She notes, "It's not only a question of seeing opportunities, it's also very much about developing them. This usually requires having the courage of your convictions and being prepared to live with the consequences. I actually think that it IS possible to develop the ability to think creatively—goodness, there are plenty of training courses about—but there is also an element of judgment, usually based on an understanding of the marketplace as well."

Françoise Bacq, a management consultant at Hewitt/CBC in Brussels, agrees with Holbeche's point that a lot of things can be learned "through a good personal development program, exactly as body-building can help train and develop a muscle."

Indeed, Bacq feels that "anyone is able to improve an entrepreneurial skill, if not to an absolute level of capacity, at least to a minimum level needed to be fit for survival. It is a question," she claims, "of need and determination and of getting the right assistance and coaching."

> *It's no good having a brilliant project if you can't sell it to anyone.*

Catie Thorburn of the Club of Brussels, an organizational think tank, isn't so sure. "Entrepreneurship is a gift," she states emphatically. And she suggests that it isn't so much Holbeche's "judgment" that counts but a factor that she calls "irresponsibility." "You have to sell yourself and your ideas, but entrepreneurs also have a degree of irresponsibility as well. You need that to have that creative zap, to take a risk. It's all a question of courage."

Thorburn goes on to point out that "people with brilliant projects never make them happen; they can't sell them to anyone. It is how you pass from the dream to the reality, how you go through all the phases of the dream and make it real. Now just how do you teach people to do that?"

Having said all that, there are people who—after examining all the other options open to them—still find themselves drawn to the dangerous life of working for themselves. But beware, not everyone can play in this game and not everyone should.

Here are a few good reasons:

- It doesn't help if you are a well-organized person if you can't sell yourself.
- It doesn't help if you know your product backwards if you can't learn to pick and choose and run your clients, rather than letting them run you.
- It doesn't help if you miss those Saturdays and Sundays on the golf course. There won't be any for a while.
- It doesn't help if you are the world's greatest salesperson but you can't get the production schedules and distribution organized.
- It doesn't help if you are the greatest programmer in software history if you can't balance the budget and keep your cash flow positive.

What You Need to Go It Alone

There's a lot more you need to have than a fax, modem, computer, and will to work. The old headhunter's phrase "All I need is a phone, a desk, and a place to hang my hat" doesn't cut the mustard anymore—come to think of it, it never did.

- You need a network, one that does superbly the last four letters—WORK—and then also provides the first three letters—as in safety NET. Don't pretend that you know lots of people; don't even believe the people you know will help you. There is a totally false saying: "When you're independent, I'll give you lots of work." If you wait for the work to materialize, you'll starve to death!
- You need to know where to get your office supplies. Don't laugh, even former senior executives have been known to fail because they never got used to the idea that they had to create and order their own letterhead.
- You need to get busy right away and have business in the bank before you start. You are not some TV private eye sitting in an office waiting for some mysterious client to appear and give you $250 a day and expenses. If you don't have a contract in writing don't start.
- Sure, you need to call the business something, but don't waste time on it. Spending a week designing a corporate logo for a one-person business is stupid. People are buying one thing—YOU. There is a simple reason why lots of successful people quoted in this book have a firm named after them. They didn't have time to waste on being needlessly creative; they just got on with it. Well done, Mr. Buzan, Mr. Ayers, Dr. Neumann, Mr. O'Shea, Mr. Muhlenhoff, Mr. Lillebo, Mr. Humble, and others.
- Continuing on that subject, never be seen as just yourself; look substantial. Whatever's happening in the field of portfolio management and the like, there are a lot of companies out there that just won't work with one-person operations or those they perceive to be that way. So, you have several choices. Be part of a network (formal, informal, or totally fictitious); have a partner; or just add associates, partners, or incorporated on your letterhead. Dressing is impressing.
- You will need help. You need a good accountant. (Don't ever get the cheapest unless you want to invest good money in your coun-

---

MANAGE SOMEONE ELSE'S STORE

If you don't think you have what it takes to be an out-and-out entrepreneur, don't despair. Catie Thorburn of the Club of Brussels suggests that there are hundreds of small and medium-sized companies
out there—many of them family owned with no successors—just
looking for senior managers with experience to take them over.

Indeed, German consultant Herbert Muhlenhoff says it is already
a major trend in his country and looks set to continue; an ideal job
for anyone who doesn't mind the transition from mega corporation
to small, entrepreneurially inclined business.

---

try's tax service.) You should also have a good lawyer and a good
person to answer the phone, fix your travel, do your research,
keep your files, and the thousand and one things that will make
you more efficient. They may be full time, overtime, part time, or
anytime they're needed, but they shouldn't be your spouse and
I don't recommend relations either.
- You most certainly need insurance. I suggest both major medical
and professional insurance. Insurance may be expensive, but if
something happens and you can't work you will be able to maintain your standard of living and that of your family.
- Finally, you need pals. Shoulders to cry on have certain criteria
attached to them. They need to be bright, intelligent, good listen-
ers, and above all pragmatic. They should not be in the business
you are in, but they should be willing to be bored to death by
your worries at a minimum of twice each year!

Now here are some things that you definitely DON'T need.

- You need a bank loan like a hole in the head. If you can get going
and keep a positive cash flow without borrowing from that big
nasty bank, do it. Incidentally, if you are setting up as a consultant
and you cannot do it without a loan from the bank, my advice is
forget it.
- The only sleeping partners you need are ones you can borrow
money from, take clients from, and learn from. Anyone who offers you all sorts of business development deals for a piece of the
action is a waste of time; they never deliver and you end up trying
to manage them to make them perform.

- You don't need a large office in a prestigious building on the best street in town. Why? Because if you are ever going to make it on your own you won't be there. You'll be seeing clients (see box on page 157 titled "Being Presentable in More Ways Than One"), in town, out of town, anywhere. If you want to work, your office should be cozy and comfortable, not impressive. The only people who need big offices are those that use them to impress—and most of them don't have jobs anymore anyway—or lawyers and advertising agencies to show you how successful they are.

Finally, there's one thing you DO need above all else—to keep your overheads as low as possible. I don't mean skimp; I mean keep them low. Yes, buy the best equipment you can—it's worth the investment. Yes, get the best tools for the job, but don't go crazy. Until you get established think frugal. There are few go-it-alone entrepreneurs who turn up in a Mercedes in the first six months of starting a new business that last the rest of the year.

A more modest view, but important nonetheless, is provided by Norwegian consultant and writer Arild Lillebo, who suggests his recipe for an individual moving from a secure job to the more uncertain world of self-employment.

- You need an attitude of realistic optimism. You won't succeed if you don't think you'll make it.
- You need time to make the change. This entails having patience, stamina, and money to pay the bills.
- You must choose a field where you know you can be competitive.
- You need to be able to tackle things that may seem below your previous status.
- You need to have a flexible organization and the ability to move easily among the files of different tasks or clients.
- You need the willingness to work long hours without expecting immediate rewards.
- You must always learn from the experience of others. Your own may be too narrow, too slow, or even too costly.
- You need to make use of and have the support of good allies who can help you on your way.

Allies are crucial and will always be so. You never run out of the need for advice, because you can never know enough, mainly because if you are successful you will never have time enough to learn everything you need to know.

> *Remember, you will never run out of the need for advice.*
> *You'll be so busy you'll never have time to learn*
> *all the things you need to know.*

From Japan, T.W. Kang, now a successful consultant after making the transition from a senior organizational position with chip-maker Intel, gives his version of getting it all together on the self-employed ski slope: "Having made the transition from a line management position as a general manager to a management consultant, I have experienced the entire process. I think that the first challenge is literally to create one's image that is saleable to multiple clients. And, unlike in the case of a manufacturing firm, that image is inseparable from the person. The second challenge, and one that relates to effective multitasking, is that one must define the business carefully so that there is a core competence that can be tailored and adapted across clients. That goes a long way to solving the next challenge, which is capacity loading. For that, time management is critical, but even more important is the art of subtly planning the peak periods when clients demand the most time so that they don't coincide with each other."

How to Structure Your Go-It-Alone Operation

But a great deal of what you do depends on how you are structured. Being an entrepreneur does not necessarily mean being on your own; there are different ways of doing it. Here are a few thoughts and observations about the ways an entrepreneur can function. Depending on your type of business and your personality, choose the one that best meets your needs.

The go-it-(a)Lone Ranger: This is the archetypal picture of the entrepreneur. If you can set aside enough time market for the future and be really disciplined about it, the it. Also, remember that you need to stay up to date and to work the market as it shifts in order to tailor your product or service unless you are cutting costs to the bone, try to make sure who can do the non-fee-would Perry Mason be without Stelappy while you are travel-earning things for you and keep cl' ing or on other assignments. Also make sure you have good back-up if jobs get too big. Being able to involve others dramatically increases your work capacity and capability. However, watch out for the sharks who say they will help you and then steal your business. In this tough world of today even people you think you know will do that. One other thing—if you couldn't manage a team when you were inside an organization, don't even try to subcontract, because you are guaranteed to screw up. There is always a downside. If you get sick there is no one else to take up the work. So make sure you are fit and carry a good professional insurance; you might never need it but you'll sleep better at night.

The Partnership: Like taking on subcontractors, two, three, four, or more like-minded people deciding to build a business increases capacity from day one, but it can breed lots of problems. Whatever happens, make sure you can get out as easily as you got in if the whole plan turns sour (a little legal investment at the beginning goes a long way later). Keep a careful note of just who is bringing in the business and make sure that the bonus system that's agreed on from the beginning is not an equal split. There will always be someone who works evenings and weekends and another who plays a lot of tennis; after a while this leads to understandable disputes. Keep the costs down (don't all go out and lease BMWs) and don't waste income on frills and fripperies. If everyone is not pulling his or her weight, don't wait around—get out fast and clean.

The Network: Networks are vastly different depending on just who is talking about them and in what context. A network can be as informal as all the people in your address book or on your Christmas card list. That's just fine, but it won't bring you a great deal of business except by accident. An entrepreneurial network is different. It can be made up of clients on one side and suppliers and information providers on the other. It can also have critical circles of close associates (people you possibly work with every day) and less critical groups (people or firms who help you out when the need arises). Creating a truly operating network that can provide assignment assistance, new leads, and lots of additional knowledge and experience is an ideal way to operate if you can manage it thoroughly. Remember one thing: just as people are part of your network, you are part of theirs. Don't forget that it's not a one-sided deal; you have to do your bit as well.

The Associates: Unlike the partnership, associates may share (as may key groups in a network) premises or be on-line to each other. The other difference is that they all charge their own fees or bill their own invoices, paying into a common fund for rentals, marketing expenses, and so on. Associates can be added to or subtracted at will and as the need arises, without causing major disruptions to the whole operation. They also provide a great source of help and comfort to the new entrepreneur.

Feeling comfortable about having a place to go to and talk about the geeks, freaks, and weirdoes that you once respectfully used to call clients is important. It will also keep you in touch with what's happening in the overall marketplace. As mentioned previously, while the Internet may be marvelous at bringing people together from all over the world, there is nothing that will ever replace being able to sit down and have coffee, a beer, or a glass of wine with a sympathetic fellow go-it-aloner.

 Go-it-aloners aren't alone ever. They see more people each day than the average nine-to-fiver does.

In fact, go-it-aloners are practically a myth. Most see more people—and a wider variety at that—than the average Joe or Jane who goes to the same office every day. That's what makes it interesting and exciting—it's new every day.

Contacts Count for Everything

Maintaining links with others is important and is obviously easier the closer you are physically, so cities still score highly with me. I know a case of a successful entrepreneurial designer—highly skilled and highly regarded—who moved just too far out from the city where most of her clients were located, to an idyllic countryside retreat. Gradually two things happened. First, she had less time to spend meeting them and keeping up with the rest of her network, so orders and commissions dwindled. Second, the change in physical proximity meant that she never saw the electronic revolution that totally changed the graphic design business. Now behind technologically, she is caught in a terrible Catch-22 dilemma. With little invested in computer hardware and software she is slower than others far less skilled and also considerably more expensive. Less work means that she cannot invest in more equipment. Keeping up with the network is a lifeline that no entrepreneur, no matter how successful, can ever forget.

Of course, not all of us have to drive ourselves to the brink to make it as a self-employed success story—especially if we know a thing or two and know people. Andrew Brown had a highly successful quarter-century career with a major international accounting company, where he was a senior partner, until an organizational reshuffle found him holding the short straw. Brown was fifty and had an excellent severance package, but he didn't want to sit around.

As a management professional with an encyclopedic knowledge of the European Union and armed with three decades of contacts— he had always been an assiduous maintainer of his network— Brown went out and put himself up for hire. As he says, "My reputation wasn't changed one bit by my new circumstances. In fact, no one referred to it."

Charging a lot less than he had in his corporate heyday, Brown now has more business than he knows what to do with and is enjoying it totally. He has learned how to run his office, juggle his clients, and keep up his knowledge, which is his product. He has eschewed adding staff, preferring to use his excellent network of contacts as he is not "desperate to make another career."

> *Make sure you have easy communications.*
> *Can you walk or bike to the bank, the travel agent,*
> *the copy shop, and the computer store?*

However, Brown not only has used his carefully nurtured network to create the perfect safety net, he has also understood the need for physical presence to both clients and suppliers. Comfortably located in Brussels, he can "cycle to the copy shop, the bank, the travel agent, and the computer shop" and has administration backup that "pops in three or four times a week."

Brown's case is the perfect example of having and getting the sense of place right—of knowing who he could turn to for work and knowing that they (because of his long-term network) knew just who he was. No doubt about it, this IS the pattern of the future for many of us—certainly all those who choose to stay small and sell our intellectual property—our experience.

HITCH UP YOUR WAGON

For those of us who don't have the urge to pit our wits and wallets in the entrepreneurial alligator pit, public relations consultant Don Bates has a suggestion. "Those who can't be entrepreneurs might be best off hitching their wagons to those who can. Generally speaking, to succeed entrepreneurs need skilled, committed people to follow their visions and ideas. One could do worse in life than follow someone in the know and in the dough!"

As Brown points out, "What you have got to consider is Who are the stakeholders in my professional life? Who are the people I need? Who are the people that care what I do?"

Learning from Entrepreneurs

We may not all make it as entrepreneurs, but we can learn a lot of lessons from them that can be put to good use in our own working world—especially that new one out there.

Indeed, Gunnila Masreliez-Steen, president of the Kontura Group in Sweden, an organizational consulting firm, thinks that, as we prepare for the next century, we should all learn as much as we can from each other's experiences and holds out an optimistic view of our collective working futures.

"People that lack knowledge about psychology and personal development usually think that everything is either there from the beginning or not possible to develop. I do not agree. After having seen people free their energy, will, lust, and courage and make new decisions about their lives, I truly believe in the power of individual change. Having said that, there are people who will never develop into entrepreneurs because they lack the ability, either through their personality or intellectually. But that doesn't cut out the rest of us. Entrepreneurs need help; they always will. If the world consisted of only entrepreneurs, no one could produce or offer the services."

She goes on, "Therefore, we need to increase the self-esteem of those other people trying to make it in an increasingly uncertain, unreliable world and understand that experts will always be needed, because experts and entrepreneurs are complementary to each other. They need each other to survive."

And survival, as we survey this changed world of work, has to be at the top of everyone's agenda. How they do that depends on their circumstances. For the new management entrant, survival will be learning to learn and getting new marketable skills. For the fast-track manager, it will be acquiring more interpersonal skills to ensure organizational survival. For those over forty-five with a large severance package and diminishing personal responsibilities, it might be a part-time job or the development of a hobby or interest into a money-making activity. For those who want the raw feeling of the ride down the rapids, entrepreneurship has many options; surviving that ride is all part of the buzz of the game but it's not for everyone.

MAKING IT ON YOUR OWN

Entrepreneurs have their own stories of how they went out on their own and how, over the years, they were able to survive, grow, and run a successful small organization. But there are some basic rules that all of us contemplating this route to earn our living should consider—simple, commonsense things that too often get forgotten.

I hope that some of my experiences in running my own business for a decade and a half may provide some insight into some of those commonsense things and save you time, energy, and worry if you decide to join those of us who took the plunge and did it our way.

Making the decision to go it alone isn't an easy one. I know that for months before I finally decided to start Johnson & Associates in 1982 I had a lot of sleepless nights and bored many close friends to death. I was choosing to leave voluntarily in a period where few people walked out of secure, well-paid, corporate jobs. As I have heard time and again from fellow entrepreneurs, their bosses urged them to stay, because it was "really hard out there on your own and you have a great future with this organization." To a man and woman they have all watched as that great corporate future they would have had vanished in a cloud of mergers, takeovers, downsizings, and bankruptcies. So the first lesson of survival is: Don't believe what people tell you. Make up your own mind. Once you have made up your mind, don't be swayed.

Make Sure You Have Business, Before You Start

Starting up an editorial services company as I did—or any service-related business—can be fraught with problems, but I think there is just one true maxim to follow: have business signed and sealed BE-FORE you begin. In my case I was able to negotiate a cast-iron, legally signed two-and-a-half-year contract with my ex-employer. At the same time I had contracted to give two days a week of time to a large communications organization to write and produce a corporate magazine as well as continuing freelance journalism assignments. Starting off in a spare bedroom (yes, overheads were kept to a minimum!), I determined to live off my ex-employer's contract and bank the rest. Thus I had no bank loans, another promise to myself I was determined to keep. Advice from an old friend put my ideas right on that. "You won't have made it, and you won't be secure until you can live for a year on your reserves," he said. Thankfully, I followed his advice, and so should anyone else contemplating life in the high-risk lane.

Be Certain You Can Multitask Your Workload

The multitask issue wasn't a problem for me. I had always done a certain amount of freelance work, both as a newspaper journalist (moonlighting for other titles) and then as a corporate executive, writing evenings and weekends. So in that case I suppose you could say I had always been entrepreneurial in outlook, always occupied with more than one employer or client. I think this is important as it teaches you how to juggle the different demands that are placed on you. This I am sure is something that any executive leaving the shelter of a company having only had a progression of single-responsibility jobs needs to think through thoroughly. He or she should spend some of that thinking time with an entrepreneur who has the experience. From a distance it can all look easy indeed. When you are open for business it is too late to find out you don't like juggling multiple demands and aren't any good at it anyway.

Technology Is Your Lifeline—Use It

Embracing and using technology—where affordable or where it could save money and time—has played a strong and continuing part in the survival of Johnson & Associates. Just six months after I began the company, the Apple II computer became widely available, though not that affordable. One of my clients asked, as we didn't do any calculating, "What on earth are you going to do with it?" He had obviously never heard of word processing. With its breathtaking 268ks of RAM it was sensational!

By 1985, there were three people and three Apple computers; later we switched to a DOS system and still later to a Windows environment. In the process we were one of the first firms in Belgium to have a group 3 fax, the machine that heralded the fax explosion. We used it mainly to transmit copy to one of our key clients, a major oil company in the United States. So new was the technology that they called us every time we sent a fax to tell us they had received it. That was less than ten years ago! From there we have progressed through scanners and design packages, mobile phones, e-mail, and whatever else would give us an edge, improve our communications, and give better service to the client. The lesson is, even if you don't pay yourself very much, always have the best equipment. Also, always try to stay ahead of the client's development. It may be expensive, but it's worth it. I have seen many organizations lose business because their technology couldn't match what the client expected. When e-mail and the Internet arrived, we actually put on a seminar for some of our clients to teach them what they were all about.

Keep Focused on What You Do Best

We have always been focused on a single core competence. In our case, words, words, and more words are our business. They might take the form of a speech for a video or a conference, an annual report, a magazine, newsletter, or book, but at the end of the day it's all words. That's what we do best. Therefore, it does pay to concentrate on what you do well and on doing it better. However, keep a close eye on change; tailor and adapt your product to that. Johnson & Associates' business has changed considerably in fourteen years by adopting new ideas and needs and adapting our skills to them.

Maximize Your Network Mercilessly

You cannot survive without a network of people you can plug into, outsource to, and generally have around to help. In our case—and we work around the world—knowing other writers, photographers, designers, and people we can rely on to find out what we don't know is vital. We have been able to create a worldwide network that can organize an interview or a photo assignment virtually anywhere. That is one of the services we offer our clients that others do not because we have set out to be international in scope. What this means is that all these people we know, respect, and trust become, de facto, our intellectual property. Currently, Johnson & Associates has five people in Brussels, with about twenty others in a close network, supported by about fifty others in a lesser network, with another three hundred or so available for occasional assignments. So you must know people; you must collect new people to replace those who retire, move out, or lower their standard of service. My product, or what Johnson & Associates offers, is my knowledge backed up by those four others in my office and those twenty, those fifty, and those three hundred. Whatever you do, guard your network well. Don't sell it short, don't give it away; it is your knowledge, it is what you can offer.

Learn to Ignore Nonconstructive Criticism

Learn to expect and accept criticism, often of the most stupid, irrational, and unconstructive kind; just smile and get on with things. Don't forget that, while you may well know your client's business inside out, you cannot always know the prevailing politics, which often have a greater bearing on the end product than any idea of relevance or quality and certainly on how much work you get. Also, people seldom really know what they want; these days often they just want it fast and for a low price. Think through whether you want to accept that as a norm for doing your business. Remember, free enterprise assumes a fair day's pay for a fair day's work; make sure you are getting that. Once you begin to compromise you can't go back and renegotiate.

Believe It—No Client Ever Stays Forever

Never fool yourself that clients stay forever. Even if you give the very best service or produce the very best product, sooner or later they will move on. In most cases it has nothing to do with you, and you are powerless to do anything about it. A new president or divisional manager with new ideas and his or her preferred supplier network is all it takes. Changes of business strategy, business downturns, and the like can do it just as well. So expect the unexpected, don't be complacent, and keep looking for new work.

Learn to Grab at Opportunities

Opportunities can appear out of nowhere. Learn to spot them and grab them; they don't sit around and wait. Likewise, learn to spot the nightmare clients and shy away from them. They are the ones that always pay late, always want more than the agreed amount of work for the same price, and those with the wrong feel to them. In these cases the customer is NOT always right. If you cannot see these people coming from a mile away, don't bother being an entrepreneur—you'll get fleeced.

Continually Evaluate Your Business

Continually evaluate the organization you have created. I chose to stay small. There will come a day when you have the opportunity to get bigger (an acquisition, a merger, internal growth). Think about it carefully and ask yourself one question: "Why did I come into this in the first place?" I did it to prove something to myself; I did it because I thought I could put my personal talents to use for organizations that needed ME; I did it to have fun and hopefully make a decent living. I've achieved all that to a greater or lesser degree. If you can feel positive that you can continue to do what you set out to do, then go ahead. But make sure you have thought it through. If you decide to stay small, be prepared to lose some clients as their needs change. Indeed, if you feel you cannot serve them in the right way, resign them—it's always better to fire a client than to have the client fire you. Finally, the day you stop having fun, get out and do something else. Hopefully, if you have followed all the advice that the people in this book have to offer, you'll know exactly what to do next.

KEY POINTS

Note: The next chapter has a complete set of checklists to help you think through your future career plans. This summary is designed to help you begin to think about the issues raised in this chapter.

1. Don't put all your savings into going it alone unless you are absolutely sure you will be good at it: the world is littered with would-be entrepreneurs who never quite made it.

2. Be careful not to confuse self-management (looking after yourself and your career) with being a go-it-alone entrepreneur: they are very different.

3. It doesn't do any good to have a great product or service if you can't sell yourself—not once but every day.

4. You must choose a field where you know you can be either unique or very competitive.

5. Your contacts—your network—count for everything.

What You Should Do Now . . .

Go to Chapter 8 and assess yourself using the checklists.

Checklists for Action

This final part of the book is designed to take a lot of the information from the other chapters and put it into checklist format, so that you can work through it and get more of an idea of what is best for you. Although the lists are not exhaustive, they should help you to gain some insight into what you personally can do and how you fit into the new world of work.

These checklists are not just for people currently looking for employment. They are good at any time to check out your ideas about the organization you work for, the organization you would like to work for, and how you as an individual shape up (Do you have an effective resume? Do you interview well? Do you want to be an entrepreneur?).

Before you begin, here are three pieces of advice.

One, answer everything as honestly as you can. There is no point in trying to fool yourself into believing you are something you are not.

Two, on the other hand, don't run yourself down. Think in a proactive manner; that's how self-help and getting in charge of YOU can best be achieved.

Three, if you can, go through your assessment with a close friend or trusted work colleague. If you are on your own when you work through it, ask someone else (preferably two or three people) if they see you the same way. Constructive criticism is a vital part of the process of learning your strengths and weaknesses.

Checklist One: Check Out Yourself

The first thing you need to know is just how flexible you really are; more to the point, perhaps, how inflexible you really are. Without understanding that, it really is impossible to begin to think about a job search with any hope of success.

1. What is your current status?

    Are you totally free to move?

    Do you have a partner with a job?

    Is he or she willing to relocate?

    Have you discussed it with him or her?

    Are you willing to relocate?

    Under what circumstances?

    Do you have children?

    Are they still living with you?

    Will a move affect any of them?

    How important is the community you live in to you? (family, friends, local associations, etc.)

Based on your responses, write down below your present availability and flexibility status.

_____

_____

_____

_____

_____

2. What are your income requirements?

    Do you own your house?

    Are your children (if any) through college?

    What assets do you have? (pensions, stocks, other savings and holdings)

    What liabilities do you have?

    Is your partner working in a secure job?

    Could you make do with less money?

    Have you discussed your financial situation with a financial advisor?

Based on your responses, write down below your current and likely future financial status.

_____

_____

_____

_____

_____

3. Just how healthy are you?

    Have you had a medical check in the last twelve months?

    Has your partner had a medical check in the last twelve months?

    Are you capable of a high (mental) stress job?

    Are you capable of a high physical stress job?

    Could you put up with considerable travel, early mornings, and late nights?

Based on your responses, write down below your current health status and how that affects your future plans.

_____

_____

_____

_____

_____

4. What are the things you really like to do?

What are the favorite parts of your work/professional life? (list them below)

_____

_____

_____

_____

_____

What are the favorite parts of your personal life? (list them below)

_____

_____

_____

_____

_____

What of these would you be prepared to give up if you had to? (list them below)

_____

_____

_____

_____

_____

What of these would you NOT be prepared to give up under any circumstances? (list them below)

_____

_____

_____

_____

_____

Based on the answers to these questions, write down below a frank, honest assessment of where you, your partner, and your family stand today, and what you would and would not do to get new employment.

Example One: "I am a totally free agent, exceptionally healthy, with no close commitments. I enjoy the challenges a job brings to me. I don't mind late nights and strange hours of work or considerable travel. My pastimes are those that allow me the maximum amount of flexibility, and I can give up or put aside nearly all of them if I need to..."

Example Two: "Being honest, home and family—as well as the local community—are the most important things to me. I have a partner with a secure but low-paying job that she enjoys, my children are practically through college, and I really don't want to go back into the stress of another corporate life-style. I would rather look after my garden and seek the right opportunity on my doorstep. My health is OK, and I have some savings that will in a few years provide for our needs..."

_____

_____

_____

_____

_____

_____

_____

_____

_____

_____

_____

_____

Checklist Two: Check Out Your Own Organization

How's your organization standing up to the stresses and strains of change? If it is doing well weathering the storms maybe you should stay with it. Equally, if it is battered and bruised it might be time to leave before you are pushed.

Take a minute or two to assess the performance of your organization on this list. If the righthand Yes column fills up more than two-thirds, run for cover! If you don't know—find out!

		No	Don't know	Yes
1.	What's the stock price trend? Is it going down?	☐	☐	☐
2.	What's the view of external commentators? Does your company get negative reports in the:			
	(a) financial press?	☐	☐	☐
	(b) trade press?	☐	☐	☐
	(c) local press?	☐	☐	☐
3.	Has the organization a recent history of downsizing?			
	(a) on a worldwide basis	☐	☐	☐
	(b) in your location	☐	☐	☐
4.	Has the organization ever stated that organizational changes were complete and then carried out others that closed plants or other facilities?			
	(a) on a worldwide basis	☐	☐	☐
	(b) in your location	☐	☐	☐
5.	Has the organization a history of less than complete disclosure of their future plans, often bringing complete surprises in its actions?	☐	☐	☐
6.	Have there been any top management departures from the organization in recent months that have not been fully explained to the staff?	☐	☐	☐
7.	Have there been any recent cutbacks in executive training and development?	☐	☐	☐
8.	Do you feel you are not being given the full support of senior colleagues and that you could perform your job better if allowed?	☐	☐	☐
9.	Has your area of operations recently downsized, leaving you with a greater level of work and increased stress?	☐	☐	☐

10. Have you been in the same position in the
    organization — without even a lateral move —
    for more than four years? ☐ ☐ ☐

11. Has your organization lost market share in any
    of its key products or services in the last two
    years? ☐ ☐ ☐

12. Is there currently a head-count freeze either
    overall or in your part of the organization? ☐ ☐ ☐

13. Has it been more than six months since you
    personally talked to the CEO of your local, national,
    or international operation? ☐ ☐ ☐

14. Do you feel that senior management comes first,
    second, and third, and the rest of the employees
    a long way behind? ☐ ☐ ☐

15. Overall, is there a negative feel to the
    operation? ☐ ☐ ☐

16. In summary, would you think that taking your
    time to look for another position now rather than
    later might be a useful option? ☐ ☐ ☐

Now, list what you like about your job and about your organization as a whole and what you don't like, and use it as an assessment of where you are now and where you would like to be:

What I like   *What I DON'T like*

_____
_____
_____
_____
_____
_____

Now, using the list you have developed, write down an assessment of your job and your organization and whether they are meeting your needs as a self-managed person.

_____
_____
_____
_____
_____

Checklist Three: Are YOU Working in the New Working World?

Is your organization, or the company you are about to join, firmly fitted into the new work contract that we all should expect?

Use the questions below to assess how well it is doing. If the righthand No column fills up more than two-thirds, activate your network!

		Don't	
	Yes	*know*	*No*

1. Do you feel that the organization you work for appreciates the new employment contract to keep you highly trained and motivated, ensuring your future employability? ☐ ☐ ☐

2. Is there a culture of positive team loyalty where the overall contribution is more important than the individual job? ☐ ☐ ☐

3. Are you encouraged to take part in multiskilled teams that enhance your overall working knowledge and reduce the compartmentalization of your job? ☐ ☐ ☐

4. Are you empowered to solve problems across departments, for customers, and so forth? Have you had adequate training to ensure that this works properly for everyone? ☐ ☐ ☐

5. Does your organization pay attention to leadership skills that have relevance to heading cross-functional/ cross-cultural teams? ☐ ☐ ☐

6. Is your organization encouraging you to learn skills outside your professional area and is it supporting this with teaching/coaching assistance or grants for that purpose? ☐ ☐ ☐

7. In your opinion, is intercompany communication open and honest, giving a true picture of the real state of the organization? ☐ ☐ ☐

8. Do you feel that top management decisions are taken with all the stakeholders (employees, customers, and stockholders) in mind? ☐ ☐ ☐

9. Is your organization focused on growth for employees, shareholders, and customers? ☐ ☐ ☐

10. Do you, or would you if you could, buy stock in the company you work for? ☐ ☐ ☐

11. Do you feel that your organization actively encourages mental and physical fitness for all its employees? ☐ ☐ ☐

12. Do you think your organization strives to achieve an exemplary standard of service both inside and outside the organization? ☐ ☐ ☐

13. Is your organization one that is constantly developing new ideas, new products, and services? Is it regarded as an innovator in its industry? ☐ ☐ ☐

14. Has your organization moved to a performance-based system of compensation that rewards people for their contributions? ☐ ☐ ☐

15. Do you feel that your organization offers and seriously cares about the quality of life of its employees? ☐ ☐ ☐

16. Compared to other organizations you know of, would you regard it as an excellent place to work? ☐ ☐ ☐

17. On the result of that assessment, could you see yourself spending a large part of your career—if that is possible—with the organization? ☐ ☐ ☐

Based on your responses, write a brief assessment of how your organization is treating you. Is it preparing you for the new working world or not?

_____

_____

_____

_____

_____

_____

_____

_____

_____

Checklist Four: Am I Fit Enough to Stay the Course?

Having assessed its attributes, let's say you want to stay with your corporation — or just want to ensure your employability elsewhere should the need arise. Here are some questions it is useful to ask yourself every so often. If the Nos in the righthand column pile up too much, maybe it's time for a long talk with yourself.

	Yes	Don't know	No
1. Are you striving to be outstanding in your present job, to really do it to the maximum of your ability?	☐	☐	☐
2. Can you show hard, measurable, long-term results that underline your ability?	☐	☐	☐
3. Do you spend time increasing your knowledge in your professional field? Are you as up to date as you can be?	☐	☐	☐
4. Have you increased your capabilities in areas outside your professional competence (e.g., completed a course in marketing or finance)?	☐	☐	☐
5. Have you fully developed your interpersonal and communication skills — and made sure top management knows about it — enabling you to lead teams and task forces effectively?	☐	☐	☐
6. Have you developed ideas that can enhance or improve the business and have you made sure these have been noted and appreciated?	☐	☐	☐
7. Do you have a good team or group of colleagues that are highly supportive and are your allies?	☐	☐	☐
8. At the end of the day are you known and appreciated as a hard, effective worker with the right skills for today's business?	☐	☐	☐

Based on your responses, write what you think you have that is unique or exceptional and relevant to today's market needs.

_____

_____

_____

_____

_____

Checklist Five: Sharpening Your Get-Out-and-Go Skills

Use this checklist BEFORE you leap into the unknown. Again, too many Nos mean you are going to have to spend quite a lot of time becoming marketable, so you had better hold onto the job. However, even if you are happy where you are, keeping up these survival skills is a must.

		Yes	*No*
1.	Have you learned anything in the past year in addition to your career-related skills?	☐	☐
	If yes, what was it? _____		
2.	Have you a personal development program?	☐	☐
	If yes, list what it is and how far you have completed it? _____		
3.	Are you an active member of any professional organizations?	☐	☐
	If yes, list the organizations and your involvement in them. _____		
4.	Are you an active member of any nonwork organizations (e.g., sports, social clubs)?	☐	☐
	If yes, list them and your involvement. _____		
5.	Have you given a speech, written an article, or been interviewed by the media in the past twelve months on a professional- or private-related issue?	☐	☐
	If yes, write down the circumstances and the outcome and follow-up. _____		
6.	Has your personal network (your contact list) increased over the last twelve months?	☐	☐
	By how much? _____		
7.	Are you aware of the current job market in your chosen business area and do you systematically keep in touch with the changing demands? If no, get started now.	☐	☐
8.	Do you, on an ongoing basis, apply for other positions in other companies to keep your interview skills sharp?	☐	☐
	If yes, how many interviews have you had in the past two years? _____		

9. Is your resume fully up to date AND well enough
    presented to get attention?   ☐   ☐

10. Are you aware of any current early retirement or
    voluntary termination program in your organization?   ☐   ☐

    If no, ask the HR department what the current situation
    is. Then, if you would consider leaving, ask them if
    there is a list for voluntary redundancy and what the
    terms and conditions are likely to be.

11. Are you aware if outplacement counseling is available to
    people leaving your organization?   ☐   ☐

    If no, find out.

12. Do you feel you are really in charge of your career and
    overall future?   ☐   ☐

    If no, spend a good deal of time working out where you
    go from here.

Now, list the items that are for you the most important to check out.

By tomorrow

_____
_____
_____
_____
_____

By next week

_____
_____
_____
_____
_____

By next month

_____
_____
_____
_____
_____

Checklist Six: Have You Got the Goods to Get Employed FAST?!

If you do find yourself suddenly unemployed there are a few things you need to be able to do for yourself quickly and without fuss. They also apply to anyone who is employed yet is looking around for a new job. Again the No column is critical: too many Nos and you had better think through your overall attitude.

		Yes	*No*
1.	Do you have an upbeat, can-do attitude? Do you see yourself getting that new job?	☐	☐
2.	Do you have an active, willing network of contacts and helpers who will be only too glad to help you in your search?	☐	☐
3.	Are you able to get over the anger and grief of not having a job quickly and put a proactive spin onto your job-search program?	☐	☐
4.	Are you capable of doing an immediate assessment of what you will need to do to get reemployed and to evaluate the current state of the job market in your business area?	☐	☐
5.	Are you able to broaden your job search and develop ideas outside your current professional/trade area and be prepared to learn about new industries in order to get a job?	☐	☐
6.	Are you fully open to new ideas and new employment options, willing to relocate if required?	☐	☐
7.	Would you be prepared to take on temporary assignments if that was what was required?	☐	☐
8.	Would you be prepared to take on what might appear to be a lesser status job?	☐	☐

Now, write down a list of the people you would call, fax, write, or e-mail.
NOTE: There is a similar listing at the end of chapter 5.

Key individuals and associations in my main network

Name	*Contact*	*Assessment of their value/support*

Individuals and associations in my secondary network

Name	*Contact*	*Assessment of their value/support*

Individuals and associations in my back-up network

Name	*Contact*	*Assessment of their value/support*

Whom should I contact? Where should I go to build up and increase my network?

Contact	*Action to take*

_____

_____

_____

_____

_____

_____

_____

_____

Checklist Seven: Checking Out the Resume

The resume or curriculum vitae should not be a list of your personal history and attributes. It should be, above all else, a selling tool. It is selling a product — YOU. It needs to be targeted, focused, and visually appealing to grab attention and able to be easily adaptable to different job applications.

Get out your resume (you should always have one handy that is up to date) and check it against the list below. Once again the Nos mean a serious reworking is in order.

		Yes	No
1.	Does your resume reflect what THEY need and not what you WANT?	☐	☐
	If no, change it!		
2.	Has anyone else ever commented on your resume?	☐	☐
	If no, get five people to look at and critique it tomorrow!		
3.	Does it highlight what you have DONE and what you can DO, pinpointing significant successes?	☐	☐
	If no, think it out and change it.		
4.	Is the first page clear and to the point? Detail can come later.	☐	☐
	If no, get six top-scoring points on the first page, clear and sharp so the reader will see them.		
5.	Is it targeted to the company you are chasing?	☐	☐
	Rifle shots work; shotguns don't!		
6.	Does it have a personalized, well-written cover letter that addresses the organization's needs and your skills?	☐	☐
	Well it should, so write one!		

7. Have you considered mailing it to more than one person
    in the organization you have targeted (e.g., CEO,
    marketing director, HR manager)?   ☐   ☐

    Don't miss out on spreading your focused message
    around an organization for want of a couple of stamps.

8. Does your cover letter show you have researched the
    company and know why you want to work there?   ☐   ☐

    If no, get an annual report, look them up in trade
    magazines, directories, and the Internet. If they
    think you cared to find out about them, chances are
    they'll want to find out about you.

Now, write down the key achievements you are the most proud of (they
don't all have to be work-related, but should be relevant), highlighting
what THEY want to see, not what YOU want.

Note: There is a similar list at the end of chapter 6.

Key achievements

_____
_____
_____
_____
_____
_____
_____
_____
_____
_____

Now, list the five you would highlight in a cover letter to go with your re-
sume. Set them down in bullet form, maximum ten words each. Examples:
"Achieved a 30 plus percent sales increase in my region in six months";
"Managed the opening of four new retail outlets simultaneously..."

_____
_____
_____
_____
_____

Checklist Eight: Getting Through the Interview

So the resume worked, you got a call, and now the next hurdle—the first interview—is looming. Check out your readiness on the list below. Again, count up the No boxes and if there are too many seek some quick-fix assistance from the professionals. Remember, interviews are not cozy chats. The objective is to sell you—not oversell you—to the prospective employer. That's all it is, so keep it neat and simple.

	Yes	*No*
1. Have you prepared for the interview by finding out as much about the company, the division, or the job on offer as you can?	☐	☐

If you want that job, just do it! Knowledgeable candidates (who don't come across like industrial spies!) get hired over the rest.

2. First impressions count: unless you are auditioning for a rock group keep it very plain Jane and John. Can you do that? Do you have a little black number (dress/suit)?	☐	☐

If no, go shopping!

3. Are you confident that you come across as a cool, confident, and competent candidate?	☐	☐

If not, consider getting professional help; interview coaching with a video can do wonders.

4. Have you discussed your interview with others (family, friends, former work colleagues)?	☐	☐

Do so — their experiences and ideas can give you information and confidence as well.

5. In the interview can you demonstrate a track record of creating and liking change and have you rehearsed your thoughts with someone to get them clear in your mind?	☐	☐

Do it—knowing your stuff is the path to employment.

6. Can you also come across as a team player and a team builder and coach?	☐	☐

Again, work at it. Stress, without forcing it, these qualities. They are what companies need these days.

7. Can you (particularly important for Europeans these days) show willingness for mixed cultural experiences—

including relocation or travel and stress experiences you
have had?   ☐   ☐

This is an important attribute; often the desire for the
experience can help immeasurably.

8. Do you talk too much?   ☐   ☐

Don't. Again get a friend to role-play the interview
process and flag you when it happens.

9. Are you aggressive when questioned too closely?   ☐   ☐

Hard as it might be, try to ignore your tendencies. Also,
don't demand guarantees or certain salaries too
early in the process. All the same, be firm; don't get
run over with your eagerness to get a job either.

10. If you have been in a job a long, long time or a very short
time, can you defend that?   ☐   ☐

Good, sound reasons work well. Being unprepared for
the question doesn't.

11. Finally, is your handshake weak, soft, and damp?   ☐   ☐

Practice a firm, confident clasp of the hands on friends.
After all, if you're hoping to work with these people,
you should feel friendly!

Now, list the things about yourself that you should emphasize and those
you should avoid. Then check them out with friends or close work colleagues to see if they agree.

Positive aspects:

_____

_____ _____

_____

_____

_____

Negative aspects:

_____

_____

_____

_____

_____

Checklist Nine: Going It Alone

If the final option for you comes down to going it alone, think your way through this list. It may not be exhaustive, but it will give you some food for thought BEFORE you take the plunge into uncertain independence.

		Yes	*No*
1.	Do you think of yourself as entrepreneurial? Have you any proof that you are?	☐	☐
2.	Ask your friends what they think. Do they consider you a Bill Gates or Steve Jobs?	☐	☐
3.	Do you have any business that you can pick up immediately?	☐	☐
	If no, think a long time before you jump in or wait until you have some.		
4.	Will you have to borrow money from a bank?	☐	☐
	Again, think long and hard about the consequences and what the loan repayments will do to cash flow and profits.		
5.	Do you like to play golf, go fishing, go drinking Saturdays and Sundays, and will you miss these activities if you can't do them?	☐	☐
	If you'll miss them, don't even start!		
6.	Are you ready to invest in technology to help you cut down your workload as much as you can?	☐	☐
	Do you know enough about the available hardware and software? If no, find out as much as you can as early as you can.		
7.	Can you be a jack-of-all-trades and do things you would not have done as an executive that might seem below your previous status?	☐	☐
8.	Can you work long hours without immediate paybacks?	☐	☐
9.	Can you juggle work so that all your clients get the full attention they think they deserve?	☐	☐
10.	Are you able to keep a focus on what you do best and not be distracted from your main goal?	☐	☐

11. Are you able to be a CEO, strategist, marketer, HR manager, financial director, and receptionist all rolled into one, every day, 365 days a year? ☐ ☐

12. Can you honestly SELL yourself and your product not once but every day and enjoy doing it? ☐ ☐

13. Can you maximize and extend your network every day? ☐ ☐

    Can you sell every day while you are working on client business? In other words, can you do three, four, or five things at once?

14. Can you ignore the wrong sort of criticism and continue to believe that you are the best? ☐ ☐

15. Can you lose clients, pick yourself up, and go find some more, and keep doing it? ☐ ☐

16. Are you capable of continually evaluating your business and doing what's right for the future by seeing and grabbing at new opportunities? ☐ ☐

17. Do you have good, trustworthy suppliers (lawyers, accountants, travel agents, etc.) who will go the extra mile for you? ☐ ☐

18. Finally, can you smell trouble and do you have an instinct for bad business deals? ☐ ☐

    If you are unable to do so, you won't make it as an entrepreneur.

Now, on the basis of your responses, do you really think you should take this idea further? Discuss it with more than one person and get a VERY honest, candid assessment before you proceed.

Bibliography

Bridges, William. *Job Shift*. Reading, Mass: Addison-Wesley, 1994.

Caudron, Shari, "HR Revamps Career Itineraries." *Personnel*, April 1994. Cites William Bridges.

Caulkin, Simon. "Take Your Partners." *Management Today*, February 1995.

Champy, James, with Michael Hammer. *Re-engineering the Corporation*. London: Harper Business, 1993.

Economic Policy Committee of the European Union. "Member States' Progress with Unemployment Policies." Brussels, 1995.

Economic Policy Committee of the European Union. "Social Benefits, Taxation and the Labour Market—Interim Report to the Council." Brussels, 13 June 1995.

Handy, Charles. *The Empty Raincoat*. London: Arrow Books, 1995.

Hutton, Will. "High Risk Strategy." *The Guardian*, 30 October 1995.

McGuire, Thomas F. "Big Barriers for Small Business in Belgium." *The Wall Street Journal–Europe*, 4 September 1995.

Patterson, Jack. *Business Week*, 17 October 1994.

Peters, Thomas J., and Robert H. Waterman, Jr. *In Search of Excellence*. New York: Harper & Row, 1982.

Smith, David. "Death Knell of the Job?" *The Sunday Times*, 19 February 1995. Cites Cary Cooper.

Stewart, Thomas A. "Planning a Career in a World without Managers." *Fortune*, 20 March 1995.

Watson, Bibi. "Omaha Takes Aim at the Work Skills Deficit." American Management Association, Fall 1995. Arbor Group report cited in this article.

Index

Advancement in a flat-structured
  company, 60-61
Advertising, recruitment, 22
  statistics on, 23
Advice for older job seekers, 138-139
Alienated employee(s), 5-6
  reasons for becoming, 5
  ridding organization of, 5-6
American way of surviving, 30-32
  big cut versus smaller cuts and, 31
  career planning and, 32
  employee-owned company and, 31
  European versus, 30
  flexibility and, 31, 32, 44
Applicants for job(s)
  arrogance and, 142
  attributes needed by, key, 140-141
  handshakes and, 141
  negative attributes of, 141
  questionnaire responses from,
    94-95, 95-96
  social skills and, 132
  standing out in crowd, pointers
    for, 121
Assessment by Human Resources of
  leaders, 77
Assessment of needs, 121
Associates, 169
Attitude changes
  employees and, 7
  job seeking and, 118, 121
  workplace and, 35-36
Attitudes about relocating, 144, 146,
  147-148
Attributes
  of future, 37
  of ideal executive, 25
  of job candidates, 140-141
  of managers, 44
  of portfolio management, 159
  of survival, 35
Armed Forces, people who leave,
  41-42

Baby-boomers and current work
  philosophy, 97-98
Bank loans and self-employment, 165
Banks and finance services, 3
Big city versus rural community,
  employees and, 10
Blue collar workers, 9
  dejobbed myth and, 130
  jobs available for, 22
  temporary work and, 45, 47
B-O-H-I-C-A, 6
Broadbanding, 78
Burger King, contract workers and, 7
Business leaders and the truth, 18, 19
Business process engineering (BPR),
  14, 16
Businesses and what you should
  know about them, 108
Buying out alienated employee(s), 5
Buzzwords, 6

Capitalism versus communism, 17, 18
Career management experts, 3
Career path
  dissolving of, 7
  severance package considerations
    for, 144
Career planning and company
  survival, 32
Career transition advice, 133-135
  accepting change and, 135
  common courtesies and, 134
  decisiveness and, 134
  decompartmentalize and broaden
    view and, 134
  executive MBA programs and, 134
  new skills acquisition and, 133
  resume updating and, 135
  self-perceptions and, 133, 134
  setting career goals and, 135
CEO. See Chief Executive Officer
Challenges to motivate employees,
  finding, 61-62

Changing job perception(s), 118, 162
Characteristics important for future, 37
Characteristics needed by prospective
    employers, 78
Charisma and job hunting, personal,
    121
Checklists for action, 178-196
    for fast employment, goods
      assessment, 189-191
    for fitness, assessment for staying
      the course, 186
    for flexibility, assessment, 178-181
    for interview survival, 193-194
    for new working world, assessment,
      184-185
    for organization you work for/hope
      to work for, 182-183
    for resume checking, 191-192
    for self-employment, assessment,
      195-196
    for sharpening your get-out-and-go
      skills, 187-188
    for survival skills, 187-188
Chief Executive Officer
    leadership and, 68
    new look of, 46
Classic victim of new working world, 5
Common courtesies and career
    transition, 134
Communication
    chief executive(s), and, 7
    flat business structure and, 67
    key piece of knowledge and, 88-89
    strategic vision and, 75
Communism versus capitalism, 17, 18
Commuting and work, 148
Companies that are excellent places
    to work, examples of, 79-80
Companies, what you should know
    about them, 108
Company characteristics one should
    look for, 78
Company person, and role today, 29
Computers and importance of for job
    seekers, 138-139, 150
Consolidation, 6
Consulting as a job option, 158
Consumer goods producers, 3
Contacts, 169-171

Contract employee. *See* Freelancers
Contracts, old versus new
    employment, 43
Core staff staying with moving
    executive(s), 29
Corporate compensation, 38
Corporate greed, 2
Corporations that are excellent places
    to work, types of, 79-80
Counseling as part of severance pack-
    age, outplacement, 121-122;
    See also Outplacement
Cover letter hints for job applicants,
    135, 136; *See also* Resume(s)
Crime build-up, 12
Cultural mobility attribute for job
    seeker, 141
Curriculum vitae. *See* Resume(s)
Customer service and downsized
    companies, 63
Cyberspace, 149, 151

Deadwood categories, 63
Decision-making ability, effective, 37
Decisiveness and career transition, 134
Dejobbed world, 21, 130
Demand-side labor market
    problem factors of, 100
    problems related to, 101
Difference between line and staff, 16
Differences looking at workplace, U.S.
    versus Europe, 30
Do now, what you should, 26-27,
    51-55, 82-84, 105-106,
    127-128, 153-154
Downsized, 2
    older employees who were, 97
Downsizing, 6
    aftermath of some, 11
    corporate fat and, 55
    customer service and, 63
    first to leave and severance package
      when, 116
    outplacement counseling and, 122
    people who go first and, 115, 116,
      117, 118
    reengineering and, 14, 15, 16, 17
    results of, 14-15
    typical example of, 117-118

Education system
impracticability of what is taught
in, 89
should include, 89
Effective decision making, 37
Elderly. *See* Older people
E-mail, 114
self-employment and, 174
young job seekers and, 140
Employee morale
downsizing and, 15-16
rebuilding, 19-22
truth telling and, 19, 20
Employee-owned company and
surviving, 31
Employers wants, 51
Employment contracts
new type of, 42-43
old versus new comparison of, 43
Empowerment, 7, 62-68, 72-73, 129
leadership and, synergy of, 73
Entrepreneurial versus self-managed,
160-163
Entrepreneurs
associates and, 169
attributes needed for, 159
checklist before becoming, 195-196
definition of, 155, 160
go-it-(a)Lone Ranger type of,
167-168
learning from, 171-176
networking and, 168, 169-171, 174
partnerships among, 168
routes to pursue before becoming,
161
successful hallmark of, 162
working for, 171
Europe and U.S. difference, 17-18,
101-102
European Union (EU), 98-99, 100,
101, 102, 170
as compared to United States,
101-102
Executive attributes
ideal types of, 25
older workers and, 51
Executive MBA programs and career
transition, 134
Executive search experts, 3, 143

Executives, "second bounce," 120

Fears of older job seekers, 145
Financial discussion during interview,
142-143
Finding challenges to motivate
employees, 61-62
Fitness to stay the course checklist,
186
Flat as requisite for today's organization, 55, 56-58, 60-61, 62
advancement from within and, 60-61
advice for becoming, 64
Catholic church as example of, 58
communication and, 67
disaster example of, 56
ingredients to making it work
and, 61
leaders effort and, 57, 68
reward process and, 78
training and, 59, 64, 67
Flexibility and survival, 31, 39, 44, 50
seeing whole picture and, 35
younger executives and, 51
Flexibility checklist, 178-181
Focus of alienated employee(s), 5
Freelance work, 12
Freelancers, 48-50, 161; *See also*
Outsourcing
people who have become, examples
of, 112

Generalist versus specialist, 45
Geographic relocation, 138, 144, 146
downsized people and, 144
reasons not to, 147-148
Government inaction, 2
Government role, 13, 18, 98-104
ideas for changing, 103
United States versus European
Union, 101-102
Growth in industry, 3
Guarantee seeking by job applicants,
141

Handshakes of job applicants, 141
Haves and have-nots, 12-19, 102
changing spread between, 39
gap enlargement of, 98

Head count and efficiency, 8
Head count myth, 11
Head-hunting industry outlook, 22
Health care, private, 12
Hired, who's getting and why,
  140-143
Human currency, 92
Human Resource assessment of
  leaders, 77
Human resource experts, 3

Ideal executive attributes, 25
Independent consultant(s). *See*
  Freelancers
Information sources on companies,
  137
Internet, 169
  networking and, 149
  self-employment and, 174
  young people using, 140
Interpersonal skills
  need of high levels of, 37, 40
  students and, 132
Interviewing, 139; *See also* Job
  applicants
  checklist for, 193-194
  videotaped mock practice for, 137
Investor greed, 2
Investors and chief executive
  communications, 7
Issues that complicate matters, 13

Japanese view of U.S. work practices,
  13, 17
Job applicant(s)
  attributes need by, key, 140-141
  checklist for determining if ready
    to be a, 189
  cover letter hints for, 135, 136
  financial discussion during inter-
    view and, 142-143
  handshakes and, 141
  improving you candidacy hints for,
    132
  negative attributes for, 141, 142
  older type of, advice for, 138-139
  responses to questionnaire by,
    94-95, 95-96
  social skills and, 132

standing out in crowd, pointers for,
  121
younger people as, 139-140
Job changes
  examples of, 111-114
  opportunities afforded by, 118
Job creation and socialist countries, 3
Job descriptions, working outside of,
  21
Job hopping, 141-142
Job interviewing. *See* Interviewing
Job market prospects, 131
Job perception, changing, 162
Job security, dissolving of, 7
Job-structure definition, changing the,
  129

Key points, 26, 51, 82, 105, 127, 153,
  177
Knowledge, 85-88; *See also* Learning
  communicating, 88-89
  goal of, 88
  horizontal and vertical types of, 88
  importance of, 2-3
  key piece of, usually missing, 88
  news and young people and, 95, 96
  power and, 115

Labor market supply-side and
    demand-side problem factors,
    100
Labor unions, 18
  government and, 103
  road blocks and, 104
Land fertility declines, 13
Large companies to small(er) com-
    panies, going from, 120,
    133-135, 165
Leaders versus managers definition,
  68
Leadership, 68, 71-79
  empowerment and, synergy of, 73
  feedback from subordinates and, 74
  instilling, 59-60
  practices of, team, 76
  qualities of, 75
  responsibility taking and, 72
  as situational, 73
  wrong hands for, 68

Learning; *See also* Knowledge
  aspects of, important, 88
  constantly, 85
  goal of, 88
  growth through, 90
  importance of, 85-88
  project work and, 37
  skills needed to be taught in school
    for, 89
  what should you be, 88-91
Leave a job, questions to determine if
    you should, 108
Legal vulnerability as reason for
    outplacement counseling, 125
Length of average executive job,
    130-131
Line and staff differences, 16

"Making the Most of Change in Your
    Career" seminar issues, 110-111
Manage someone else's store, 165
Management
  firing of employees by, reason
    for, 4
  incentives for lying to workers
    by, 3-4
  stock option bonuses for, 4
  truth telling and, 3-4
Management credibility, 7
Manager's mind-set, changing, 23-25
  examples of, 119
Managers
  attributes now needed for, 44
  ex–Armed Forces people as, 41-42
  feedback from subordinates and, 74
  renaissance type of, 97
  women as, 65-66
Managers versus leaders definition, 68
Mantra examples for coping in
    business, 146-147
Manufacturing, heavy, 3
Mean as a requisite for today's
    organization, 55
Mega corporation future, 59-60
Mental attitudes of victims of change,
    10, 120-121
Mentors, 113-114
Middle class
  declining, 13

  work revolution and, 8-9
Middle management
  cuts affecting, 8-9
  passing on of false hopes and, 4
Mind-set, changing, 23-25, 91, 118
  examples of, 119
Mission statements, 69, 71
  examples of, 69-70, 70, 71
Morale, 7
  addressing of, 61
  downsizing and, 14-15
  employee, rebuilding, 19-22
  outplacement counseling and, 125
  truth telling and, 19, 20
Movement within a flat-structured
    company, 60-61
Moving
  companies, 8
  employees, 8, 10
Multidisciplinary skills, 44, 45, 66
Multidisciplinary teams, leading, 41;
    See also Flat as requisite for
    today's organization
Multinational giants and their future,
    59-60
  benefits of working for, 60
Multitasking and self-employment, 173

Networking, 109-115, 137, 140
  corporate headquarters contact and,
    114
  e-mail and, 114
  importance of, 109, 131, 174
  Internet and, 149
  self-employment and, 164, 168,
    169-171, 174
  young people and, 140, 150
New blood as incentives to alienated
    employee(s), 6
New skills acquisition and career
    transition, 133
New-working-world checklist, 184-185
News and knowledge of by young
    people, 95, 96

Office supplies for self-employed, 164
Older people
computers and importance of for
    job seeking and, 138-139

Older people, *continued*
 downsized and employment for, 97
 excepting change and, 36
 executive attributes and, 51
 fears about job hunting and, 145
 job-seeking advice for, 138-139
 peaking time of, 117
 relocation by, 144, 145, 146
 survival skills and, 35
 temporary work and, 46, 47
Organization-of-today description, 55
 key words, 55, 82
Organization performance checklist,
  182-183
Organizational dysfunctionalities, 7
Outplacement/outplacement
  counselors, 126
 buying out alienated employee(s)
  and, 5
 downsizing and, 122
 experts in, 3
 image of company as reason for,
  125
 importance of, 122, 137
 legal vulnerability and, 125
 morale and, 125
 self-employment discussions with,
  156, 157
 severance package and, 121-122
 timing for, 124-125
Outsourcing, 20; *See also* Freelancers
 ex-employees and, 33
 peripherals of, 32-33
 rise of, 22-23

Partnerships, 168
Paying more to fewer people, 4
Peak productivity time for people,
  117
People-cutting exercises, 4
People management skills, 37
Periodicals commenting about new
  world of work, 6
Philosophies and values to live by,
  67, 69-71
 examples of, 69-70, 70-71
 mantra example for, 146-147
Pillars of Western existence and
  workplace, 8

Places to work that are excellent,
  examples of, 79-80
Political militants, 13
Politicians and truth, 18
Portfolio management, 158, 159, 160
 attributes needed for, 159
 one-person operations and, 164
Practical skills and schools, 89
Priority changes in employees, 7
Proactivity, 21
Problem-solving ability, 37
Productivity goals and alienated
  employee(s), 6
Project work as learning
  experience(s), 37
Prospects for tomorrow, assessing, 2
Pyramid rebuilding, 11

Qualities of leadership, 75
Questionnaire responses by job
  applicants, 94-95, 95-96
Quitting a job, questions to determine
  if you should, 108
 checklist for, 187-188

Racism, 13
Rebuilding employee morale, 19-22
 truth telling and, 19, 20
Recruitment advertising for jobs
  outlook, 22, 23
Reengineering, 6, 14-17, 50, 55, 56
 downsizing and, 14
 example of, 58
 looking for, prospective employers
  and, 78
 original intention of, 14
Religious radicalism resurgence, 13
Relocating
 attitudes about, 144, 145, 146
 companies and, 8
 employees and, 8, 10
 geographically, 138, 144
 reasons not to, 147-148
Renaissance manager, 97
Reorganization, 6
Responsibility taking, 72
Resume(s)
 checklist for, 191-192
 contents of, 136-137

Resume(s), *continued*
  executive search consultants and
    unsolicited receipt of, 143
  object of, 136
  targeting the, 136, 139
  test marketing your, 137
  updating and career transition, 135
Rewarding flexibility, 44
Ridding organization of alienated
    employee(s), 5-6
Rightsized, 2
Rural community versus big city,
    employees and, 10

Sabbaticals, 119, 120
Salary concerns, reevaluating, 113
Schools
  impracticality of what is taught in,
    89
  what should be taught in, 89
Search consultants, executive, 143
Search for excellent place to work,
    79-81
"Second bounce" executives, 120
Security, pointers to get additional,
    109
Self-employment, 155-177; *See also*
    Entrepreneurs; Freelancers;
    Portfolio-management
  attributes needed for, 159
  bank loans and, 165
  before starting, 172-173
  checklist before becoming, 195-196
  client-base changes and, 175
  company name and, 164
  considerations for, 161
  contacts and, 169-171
  criticism handling and, 175
  evaluating your, 175-176
  factors against becoming, 157, 158
  focusing on what you do best and,
    174
  go-it-(a)Lone Ranger type of,
    167-168
  help factors for, 164, 165
  insurance and, 165
  multitasking and, 173
  needs for being, 164-167

  networking and, 164, 168, 169-171,
    174
  not needed for, 165-166
  office supplies and 164
  offices of, 166
  reasons against becoming, 163
  recipe for, 166
  structuring, 167-169
  technology and, 173-174
  time management and, 167
Self-managed definition, 160
Self-managed versus entrepreneurial,
    160-163
Self-perceptions and career transition,
    133, 134
Self-protection of employees, 7
Sense of community and workplace, 8
Severance
  career changes and, 144, 146
  package for first to leave during
    downsizing and, 116
  sabbaticals and, 119
  self-employment using, 156
Shareholder(s)
  management communication
    with, 7
  profit demands by, 4
Skills to operate effectively, 35
  key, 37
  sharpening checklist for, 187-188
Social crisis, reasons for, 2
Social organization, workplace as, 8
Social skills and job candidates, 132
Sources of information on companies,
    137
Specialist versus generalist, 45
Staff and line differences, 16
Streamlining, 6
Structuring your self-employment
    business, 167-169
Students
  attitudes about jobs and, 96
  responses to job application
    questionnaire and, 94-95, 95-96
Supermanagers, 41, 49
Supply-side labor market
  efficiency problems of, 100-101
  problem factors of, 100

Survival
    options, 172
    skills checklist for, 187-188
Surviving and mental attitude, 10
Surviving the American way, 30-32

Talking too much as job applicant,
    141
Taxes, 100, 101, 103
    government incentives and, 103
Teaching transferable skills, 93
Team builder as attribute for job
    seeker, 141
Team leadership practices, 76
Teams, working in, 37
Technology and alienated
    employee(s), new, 5-6
Technology and self-employment,
    173-174
Teleworking, 151, 153
Temporary work
    attitude changes about, 47
    blue-collar workers and, 45
    managers and, 45-48
    older worker and, 46
Tenets of business example, 70, 71
Tenure length of average executive
    job, 130-131
T-form manager, 32-35, 36, 41, 51,
    160
    definition of, 34
Time management and
    self-employment, 167
Time span considerations at a job,
    141, 142
Training, 59-62; *See also* Learning
    attracting best people and, 91
    flat companies and, 64, 67
    forms of, 91
    programs and, 40
    roles and responsibilities
        knowledge and, 66
    thinking type of, 90-91
Transferable skills, teaching, 93
Transition advice, career, 133-135
    accepting change and, 135
    common courtesies and, 134
    decisiveness and, 134

decompartmentalize and broaden
    view and, 134
executive MBA programs and, 134
new skills acquisition and, 133
resume updating and, 135
self-perceptions and, 133, 134
setting career goals and, 135
Transitional roller coaster diagram,
    124
Travel considerations, world, 142
Truth from politicians and business
    leaders, 18, 19
Types of corporations that are
    excellent places to work, 79-80

Unconventional manager, 44-45
Unions; *See also* European Union
    government and, 103
    road blocks and, 104
United States and Europe difference,
    17-18
    European Union and, 102-103
United States Armed Forces, people
    who leave, 41-42

Values and philosophies to live by,
    69-71
Victim of new working world, classic,
    5
Victims of change and mental attitude,
    10
Videotaped mock interviews, 137

Wants of employers, 51
War and workplace correlations, 9-10,
    12
Water shortages, 13
Western Europe and job creation, 3
What should you be learning, 88-91
What you should do now, 26-27,
    51-55, 82-84, 105-106,
    127-128, 153-154
White-collar workers, losing of jobs
    by, 2
Who's getting hired and why, 140-143
Women as managers, 65-66
Work ethic, 91-93, 94, 95, 96
    money and, 95

Workplaces that are excellent, types
    of, 79-80
Workplace
    attitude changes and, 35-36
    looking at, U.S. versus Europe, 30
    social organization and, 8
    war zone and, 9-10
World market emergence and CEOs, 9
World travel considerations, 142

World Wide Web versus in-person
    contact, 150
Writing skill and importance of, 132

Younger people
    advice for the future for, 150-151
    learning skills and, 36
    letter writing by, 139-140
    relocating and, 147-148